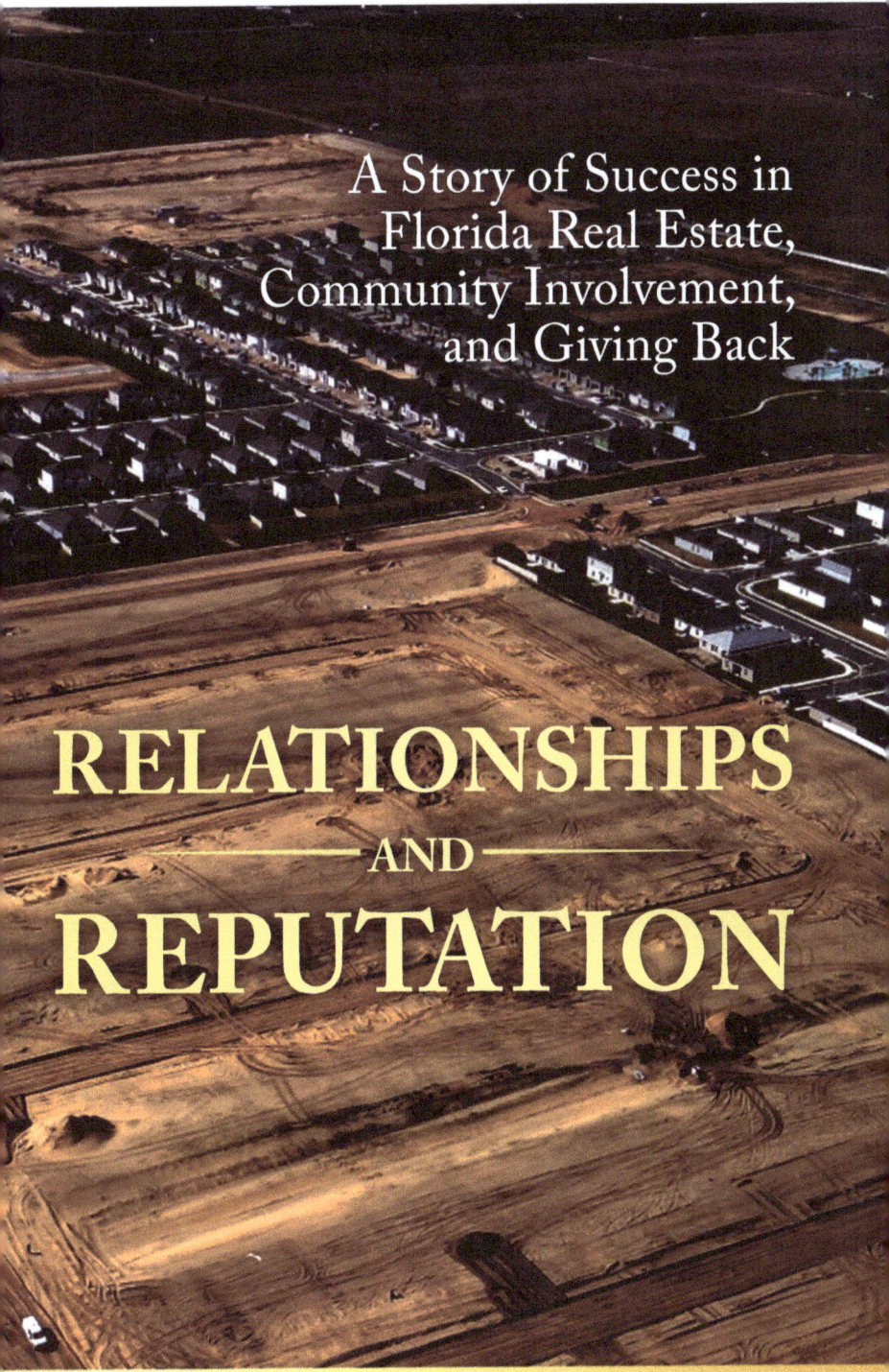

A Story of Success in
Florida Real Estate,
Community Involvement,
and Giving Back

RELATIONSHIPS
— AND —
REPUTATION

ALLAN E. KEEN

Copyright © 2025 by **Allan E. Keen**

All rights reserved. No part of this book may be reproduced, distributed, or transmitted in any form or by any means, including photocopying, recording, or other electronic or mechanical methods, without the prior written permission of the publisher or author, except in the case of brief quotations embodied in critical reviews and certain other noncommercial uses permitted by copyright law.

Paperback ISBN: 978-1-956464-58-0
Hardcover ISBN: 978-1-956464-59-7
First Edition 2025

This publication is intended to provide accurate information on the subject matter covered. It is sold with the understanding that neither the author nor the publisher offers legal, investment, accounting, medical, or other professional advice. The author and publisher make no representations or warranties regarding the accuracy or completeness of the contents and expressly disclaim any implied warranties of merchantability or fitness for a particular purpose. No warranties may be extended by sales representatives or materials. Professional consultation is recommended as individual circumstances vary. Neither the author nor the publisher shall be liable for any damages, including but not limited to loss of profit, incidental, or consequential damages.

Published by BrightRay Publishing
https://brightray.com/

To my wife, Linda:
*Your loyal support, love, encouragement,
and remarkable mothering
and care for our two daughters made my success possible.*

**To Rollins College and the Crummer Graduate School
of Business at Rollins:**
*Without the opportunities you gave me at the beginning,
I may have become a sharecropper in Mississippi, and my success
would have been much more difficult to achieve.*

TABLE OF CONTENTS

Chapter 1:	W-2 Paycheck	1
Chapter 2:	Good Fortune	9
Chapter 3:	Barnett Bank	17
Chapter 4:	The Winter Park Jaycees	25
Chapter 5:	Two-Week Notice	29
Chapter 6:	Real Estate License	33
Chapter 7:	Opportunity One—Euro Capital Partners	41
Chapter 8:	Opportunity Two—Universal Studios	45
Chapter 9:	The Keewin Real Property Company	53
Chapter 10:	Exclusive Broker	61
Chapter 11:	The Elizabeth Morse Genius Foundation	65
Chapter 12:	Windsong	73
Chapter 13:	External Forces	77
Chapter 14:	The Expressway Authority	85
Chapter 15:	The Alfond Inn	93
Chapter 16:	Mister Rogers	103
Chapter 17:	The Kummer-Kilbourne House	113
Chapter 18:	Faith, Family, and Friends	119

Afterword 129
Acknowledgments 137
Notes 143
About the Author 147

CHAPTER 1
W-2 PAYCHECK

"Though I cannot describe an intended path to success, I have identified two enduring themes that have been present and resonated throughout my career: relationships and reputation."

When I took a career path in business, there was not an entrepreneurial bone in my family's history. In fact, no family member had ever attended college.

My father, Vernie Keen, was somewhat of an introvert. He achieved success in the retail/grocery industry, but he mostly kept to himself, never becoming involved in community activities. At the age of 17 in Savannah, Georgia, he began work as an assistant in the meat department for an Atlanta-based grocery company called Colonial Stores. In a covered shed behind that grocery store, he and other associates would butcher and prepare meat that would be sold in the display cases at the front of the store. Carving meat carcasses, the employees would throw the scraps onto the sawdust-covered floor. While the sawdust made for simple cleanup later, it also created a particular cat problem. With the scraps of meat soaking into the sawdust, stray felines saw the shed as a two-in-one paradise. Not only did the sawdust make for excellent cat litter, but the meat trimmings also served as tasty treats, far better than the other stuff they had to eat. As you can imagine, my father quickly developed a dislike for cats, an animosity that lasted even after he left the job. Only years later would he come to like cats again.

Over the next 30-plus years, my father rose in the ranks to assistant meat manager, meat manager, assistant store manager, store manager, district manager, and then regional manager. His climbing the ladder was only paused during WWII when he served in the US Army until 1948. After his military service, when he accepted a job as a regional manager, the company expanded and built grocery stores in Virginia, where he, my mother, and my brother moved—and where I was born in Newport News later that year. He stayed in this position for another decade until the late 1960s when the US government began debating pension rights in Congress, partially as a result of the New Deal.

The National Pension Plan determined that when a company set up a pension plan, its employees would contribute five years' worth of "back" pension payments, while the company would be required to contribute the remaining years for all prior years of service. For example, if an employee worked at the company for 25 years, the employee would be required to contribute to the pension for five years, and the company would pay for the other 20 years. However, this meant that for companies with many long-serving employees, the potential pension liability posed a significant financial threat. If large numbers of workers agreed to join the plan, the company would have to pay decades and decades' worth of past pension contributions all at once, which could potentially bankrupt a business if the numbers were too large.

In an effort to offset this potential liability, the US government offered a one-time exemption where, for a brief period of time, a company could terminate long-serving employees and replace them with new hires, which would dramatically reduce or eliminate the pension contribution liability and ease the financial impact on the company. Taking advantage of that exemption, Colonial Stores let go of close to 100 employees—from the president of the company to many district and regional managers, including my father. After 33 years of loyalty and service, my father found himself fired from his position as the regional manager for the Colonial Stores located in Virginia.

At the same time, another regional grocery chain was growing in the state of Mississippi: Lewis Grocer Corporation, which operated under the brand of Sunflower Stores. Because the company wanted to expand even quicker, it approached many of the senior executives who had been let go by Colonial Stores. Although he spent a six-month stint in Jackson, Mississippi, with the new company, my father decided that he did not want to move the family to Mississippi, and he began looking for other employment opportunities.

While my mother was the extrovert in the family, she was also a homemaker, for the only job she ever had was being a good wife and taking care of my dad, brother, and me. Therefore, as I entered the seventh grade and my brother the eighth, she did not object when my father signed up for a job in Puerto Rico. Based on a friend's recommendation, he decided to move the family there in 1960. He didn't call a "family meeting" to discuss the decision, weigh the pros and cons, or hear anyone's opinions about the matter. My father made the choice, arranged the travel plans, and had us follow—not in a dictatorial way, but rather because he knew it was the right thing to do at the time. My dad was not a risk-taker, but he recognized that this move could be a unique experience and opportunity for him and us. So, we packed our bags and boarded a flight to San Juan.

Río Piedras, the town where we lived, was a populous suburb of San Juan. Our single-family, ranch-style house was located in a middle-class neighborhood with other typical families, almost all of whom were locals and primarily spoke Spanish, a language my brother and I did not speak.

My brother, Tim, was only a year and a few months older than me. He did not have much to do with me until we moved to Puerto Rico. Since we knew no one there, we were forced to hang around together. Back in Richmond, where we lived prior to moving, he had his own friends, and I had mine. Tim hung around boys older than him, so despite our small age gap, he always acted more grown-up than I did. However, in Puerto Rico, we had few, if any, English-speaking friends. During this time, and even into high school, I did not play sports or have a part-time job; instead, I spent most of my time with my brother, who quickly became my best friend.

Right before I entered the 10th grade, our father decided to move us back to the mainland US to Orlando, Florida, wanting us to have a better chance to attend an American college by graduating from a US high school. Looking back, I can say that those three years in Puerto Rico matured me—a noticeable change when my family returned to the US. Most young people do not grab hold of their "free will" until later in college, but life in Puerto Rico was freer and more open with few restrictions. This environment gave me more control over my choices at an early age and provided the basic foundation for the way I navigated major decisions. Because of my "growing up" early in Puerto Rico, as a 16-year-old boy in Orlando, I did not spend time trying to get my hands on a can of beer or wondering when I could attend the next party; rather, my independence, which later defined my life path, began to develop.

In my senior year at Colonial High School, right around Christmas, my father's job at a small, local grocery store in Orlando did not work out, and he began to reconsider the job opportunity in Mississippi. His co-workers from Colonial Stores, many of whom now worked for Sunflower Stores, had solicited him to join them in Mississippi over the prior four years. Not only did they like him, but they knew he had great talent.

As Tim and I were approaching college age and preparing to move out on our own, our parents moving to Mississippi luckily did not impact us much. However, my father still hesitated to accept Sunflower's offer. For starters, he was in his late 50s. With decades of experience, to take a job that was not commensurate with his skills weighed on his pride. Being close to retirement age, making this move almost felt like starting from scratch. The people who had once worked for him had been with this new company for four years, meaning they would be in higher positions than my father. He would go from being their boss to being their employee, near the bottom of the proverbial totem pole, which was a bit hard to accept.

As my father continued to resist the potential move, he instead took on menial jobs for several businesses, some small and others large. His career, with more than three decades of hard work, turned into this-and-that odd jobs around Central Florida. At one point, he even became a door-to-door salesman, walking around neighborhoods, knocking on doors, and selling

AAA family memberships—a task well below his skill level and experience. This had an immense and negative impact on his pride and self-esteem. As his colleagues at Sunflower Stores continued to reach out to him, the hit to his dignity finally caused him to give in, take the job, and move to Mississippi with my mother. The company would give him a good opportunity and pay him well, and he certainly knew how to execute the job requirements to a high standard. Selling AAA family memberships in Tampa could not pay the bills, for each sale would have earned him only about $20 in commission!

Looking back on my father's story and his age as he experienced a major career change, I consider my own career. As almost anyone can tell you, I have never been a serious planner, even when planning my own business. Many young people throughout my career, especially those interested in the real estate business, have approached me asking for advice on how to be successful. The question is not an easy one to answer. While I could attempt to create a "10-step plan" on how to follow the correct life path, the truth is that I have been extremely fortunate in my career to meet the right people and to sit at the right tables. And although there are reasons why I have taken certain paths and made specific business decisions, many opportunities resulted from happenstance, luck, or taking action when the chance arose. This is the major topic of this book, from which I hope others can benefit.

Though I cannot describe an intended path to success, I have identified two enduring themes that have been present and resonated throughout my career: relationships and reputation. Because of the relationships I have formed, both with individuals and with others in the community, and the reputation that I have established for myself, I have had the good fortune and financial stability to not have received a single W-2 paycheck since December 15, 1973. I sincerely believe that if someone takes these priorities to heart and accepts them as core principles, they and the community around them, more often than not, will be better off for it.

CHAPTER 2
GOOD FORTUNE

"I simply wanted to be successful. Not a millionaire with X number of dollars, but just successful."

Prior to my father accepting the position in Mississippi, I registered to attend the University of South Florida, expecting to live with my mother and father in Tampa. Although I was accepted to USF, the scholarship I received only covered my attendance as a day student, and with my father now taking the Sunflower Stores position, I no longer had a place to live there. I was already living with a friend in Orlando for the last three months of my senior year so that I could graduate from my high school.

Delta State College (now Delta State University) in Cleveland, Mississippi, seemed like the next logical option since it was about 36 miles north of Greenville. Very shortly after I applied, the college awarded me a full academic scholarship for all four years, again as a day student. As the world handed me my next opportunity, I accepted. Back then, high school graduates rarely applied to more than one college, so when I chose Delta State, that decision would normally have been etched in stone.

The fact that I would go to Delta State was all that I reasonably could have expected and be thankful for.

Just as I was about to graduate from Colonial High School, a surprise opportunity once again changed my life path: Rollins College in Winter Park was looking for 15 to 20 local students from Central Florida as part of a plan to diversify the student body, as many of its students came from other states, particularly from the Northeast and Midwest.

The high school guidance counselors considered my grades in response to the announcement. I had never visited my high school guidance office before, never having any reason to do so since I kept myself out of trouble and made good grades, when one of the school counselors approached me with the opportunity to attend Rollins. The college offered me a full-ride, four-year scholarship—but once more, as a day student.

With no place to stay in Orlando or Winter Park, my initial thought was that I would have no choice but to decline the offer. Colonial High, after hearing that I had been offered a full scholarship to attend Rollins, recognized this as a prestigious honor and wanted to assist me in becoming a student there. The guidance office proposed a solution: The head of the home economics department at my high school, Mrs. Elizabeth Harrington, and her elderly husband needed assistance around their house, and if someone was willing to help with chores and other tasks, they would offer free housing.

Not taking any time to decide, I took them up on their offer.

At the beginning of my freshman term at Rollins in August of 1966, I moved into their spare bedroom with no personal belongings other than a few suitcases of clothes. The "help" the Harringtons needed, as I found out, involved cutting the grass, grocery shopping, and other chores mainly involving physical labor—all of which I did not mind doing, especially for a free room and free dinners.

Mrs. Harrington was about five-and-a-half feet tall. She liked to eat her own cooking, and as the head of the home economics department at the high school, she excelled in the kitchen. Hailing from Dothan, Alabama, she whipped up Southern cornbread, pork chops, and pies with care and intention, ensuring I would never go to bed with an empty stomach. Even though I lived without restrictions for the most part, with my parents being hundreds of miles away, I still considered Mrs. Harrington's house my home. She quickly became a second mother to me, so much so that my friends and I even began referring to her as Mom Harrington.

Mrs. Harrington's husband lived for approximately two years after I moved in, as he was about 30 years older than her. Shortly thereafter, she sold their house and moved to two different apartment complexes over the next few years, and I moved with her. I lived with her for a total of five years, the amount of time it took for me to complete both my bachelor's degree and MBA from Rollins, and after moving in, like most college students, I only went back home to Mississippi for Easter and Christmas.

When first applying to college, my inclination was either to study Spanish—an easy way out as I already knew the language from my time in Puerto Rico—or one of the humanities, such as history or English. Business never crossed my mind as an option.

However, as fate would have it, I never had the chance to sign up for Spanish, English, or history. In fact, I initially could not sign up for anything because, for some reason, I showed up late for my freshman orientation and registration. *One day* late.

I was upset, not knowing how this could have happened, for I have always been an "early bird." Arriving late seemed highly uncharacteristic of me.

"I'm sorry to say," the college admissions representative informed me. "All of the freshman faculty advisors have already been assigned."

A skinny, fresh-out-of-high-school 18-year-old, I did not know what that meant.

"Does that mean I can't go to college?" I asked, thinking I had just blown it.

"No, no, no! We'll find someone to be your freshman advisor," the staff member reassured me. "Don't worry about it."

How it happened, I have no idea, but Rollins did secure a freshman advisor for me ... and they picked a very unexpected choice—Dr. Charles Welsh, the dean of the Crummer Graduate School of Business. Not simply an undergraduate business professor, but the *dean* of the MBA school.

Before this, I never would have imagined that I would seek a business degree, let alone an MBA. But as soon as Dr. Welsh became my freshman advisor, my life path changed, and I enrolled in the 3/2 MBA program, meaning that I spent my first three years at Rollins as an undergraduate with the last two years at Crummer, earning my MBA. Furthermore, because accreditation agencies at the time did not allow colleges to have both bachelor's business degree programs and MBA programs, Rollins did away with its undergraduate business degree. Instead, advisors prompted MBA students to pick an undergraduate track that would relate to their future interests as a businessperson, whether that be software engineering, communications, education, or another broader pursuit. Not seeing how my aforementioned plan for English or Spanish would help me alongside a master's degree, I instead chose to major in economics.

A Portrait of Dr. Charles Welsh

Economics coursework, involving statistics, theory, and other related materials, came easily to me. Of course, I studied hard, but I never struggled to make an A, only ever earning one sub-A grade in my entire college career after failing a chemistry test near the end of my freshman term. For the first three years, I took a full load of classes and worked about 40 hours per week for room and board, so I was not one to partake in stereotypical college parties or get into any trouble. I did not have the time or means to "raise hell" like some college kids; instead, I had to try my best to be successful in everything I did.

Even then, there was an aspect of college life that I did struggle with: making ends meet. My family could only afford to send me $10 a week—my only support and source of income, for which I was grateful. Until my junior year, I did not have a job other than my work-study at the college library, and it was only when I entered my senior year that I opened my first checking account. Up to that point, I had no money to put in it.

My financial situation came up again during my senior year when my accounting professor approached me and asked, "Have you ever invested in the stock market?"

This accounting professor worked at the graduate level in the Crummer Graduate School of Business, and I had enrolled in two of his classes. It may also be important to note that I was never one to knock on a professor's office door to chit-chat. As a working student, I never had the time—not that I had any problems to discuss with my professors anyhow. So, I cannot remember now why I was called in to that professor's office, only that his question surprised me.

"No, sir," I responded. "I don't have any money to invest."

The professor told me not to worry about that, instead recommending that I buy two real estate investment trusts: Barnett Bank REIT and Barnett Winston REIT. Both investments related to my workplace at the time, Barnett Bank of Winter Park, which may have precipitated the conversation, though I had no clue as to why he was suggesting this to me. This professor and I were not meeting for drinks or discussing money as good friends when he proposed the idea. However, while the conversation seemed out of the ordinary, I also recognized that I was a good student who had an interest in Barnett Bank and its related entities. So, when he lent me $5,000 to try investing for the first time, I did not turn down the opportunity.

The investment process was more complex in the 70s, and purchasing a stock required more steps than it does today. With my $5,000 loan, I went to the bank and opened a brokerage account. Then, I called a stockbroker, who made the two stock purchases on my behalf. I do not remember how I ended up selling the stocks, only that I made a small profit of about $1,000 over nine months, after returning the original loan amount with interest to my professor. While this accounting professor did not continue to loan me investment funds, he did educate me about how to invest and show me how I could profit. I believe this was his way of introducing me to the investment business, a side of finance I likely would not have involved myself in until much later in life had he not encouraged me to do so.

I spent my time in college following similar opportunities, but despite the individualized support I received as a student at a small liberal arts college, the majority of my motivation came from somewhere deep within me. My family provided little moral support, for everything I did, from finishing high school to enrolling in college to later starting my career, I did on my own, greatly due to the relationships I built and maintained with others.

Unlike some peers in my classes, I did not have a family business to run or an entrepreneurial passion I wished to pursue. I simply wanted to be successful. Not a millionaire with X number of dollars, but just successful. From the ages of 20 to 40, I had the drive to build relationships and create a path to success for the rest of my life. Past my 40s, I anticipated achieving the financial "success" part of my goal. Then, from 60 onward, I would "possibly" retire and donate to philanthropic causes, a part of my life goals that seems intrinsic to my DNA. It is rare to have a detailed life plan in college, and I was no exception. I did have a destination in mind but didn't know which road I needed to take.

What I could not foresee was the continued good fortune that changed the direction of my life, most of which stemmed from the opportunities and relationships that I created as a student at Rollins. What the college did for me and my personal development cannot be overstated. Had I attended another college, like Delta State, who knows where I would be today? I could have been the governor of Mississippi, or maybe I would have been a sharecropper. Rollins deserves immense credit, appreciation, and thanks for reaching out to me, accepting my application, presenting me with many opportunities and relationships, and influencing my career well beyond my collegiate tenure, specifically in two major instances. Rollins, in addition to the academic classes and learning opportunities, made it easy to contribute and give back through community service and countless other endeavors.

While there, I learned public speaking, and I learned how to manage time. Most importantly, I learned about community service and what those words truly mean. And somewhere in that process, the impetus to give back—a calling that has followed me for the majority of my life and shaped most of my most pivotal choices and successes—somehow came to be. This compulsion was not planned or calculated. Rather, it guided my next moves, always returning me to the pivotal question: How can I make an impact?

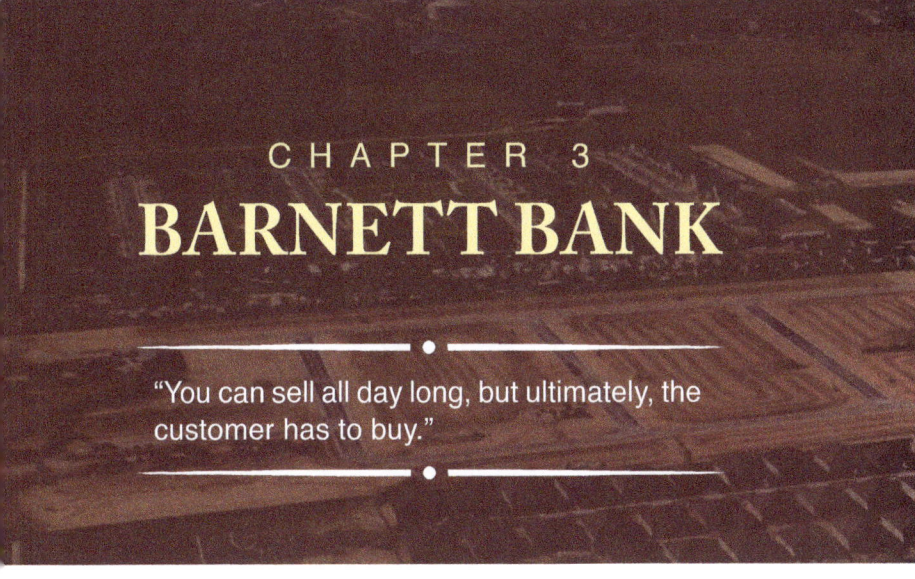

CHAPTER 3
BARNETT BANK

"You can sell all day long, but ultimately, the customer has to buy."

I worked at the library on Rollins's campus for my first two years in college, but during my third year, Dr. Charles Welsh, as the dean of the Crummer School and my faculty advisor and mentor, encouraged me to apply for a scholarship with the Florida Bankers Association (FBA).

The application required candidates to list a recommending banker and a hometown banker as references. Although my mother and father had lived in Greenville, Mississippi, for several years, they did not know of any bankers to put on my application.

Dean Welsh was close to the president of what was then called First National Bank of Winter Park (later Barnett Bank). It was there that I met my second important mentor, Charles "Charlie" Rice, the president of the bank and a Crummer graduate.

Bankers are often stereotyped as serious and formal. Charlie had these traits, but he was also charismatic and outgoing, very different from the academic personality of Dr. Welsh.

Well-known and well-liked, Charlie became president of Barnett Bank at 35 years old, a young age for his position. He knew what Dean Welsh was doing for me, being my advisor and introducing me to the FBA scholarship opportunity. On Dean Welsh's recommendation, Charlie Rice, who was also a member of the FBA scholarship committee, agreed to become both my recommending banker and my hometown banker on the application. With that support, I was awarded the money by the FBA.

This financial support wasn't technically a "scholarship"—it was actually a grant/loan. Recipients would be awarded $10,000 per year for two years, and it would be forgiven if the recipient worked at a Florida bank for two years after graduation. Once I was a recipient and part of the program, I was introduced to four banks for part-time employment: Barnett Bank, First National Bank of Orlando (SunBank/Trust Bank), Florida National Bank, and the Commercial Bank of Winter Park.

After visiting each bank and talking to its respective leadership, I was offered a job as a drive-in teller at the Commercial Bank of Winter Park. At the same time, Charlie Rice offered me a job in the mailroom at Barnett Bank. While I certainly wasn't too proud to work in the mailroom, I thought I'd rather sort money over mail. So, even though I owed my scholarship to Charlie Rice's efforts, I took a job with the Commercial Bank of Winter Park and worked there during my junior year.

During the early part of my senior year, a bank officer from Commercial Bank moved to Barnett at the very beginning of the bank credit card era. Before this, the only credit cards were T&E (travel and entertainment) cards, available through companies such as Diners Club, Carte Blanche, and American Express. So, when banks began issuing credit cards, Barnett Bank, due to its multiple locations and influence around the state, became the exclusive bank in Florida to issue BankAmericard, which later became Visa in 1976.

I became acquainted with an officer at Commercial Bank, George Foster, who had previously worked at a major bank in Atlanta that had pioneered the bank credit card. Barnett Bank, interested in building out its own credit card program, recruited George to start its credit card department. Shortly after he arrived, he went to Charlie Rice and requested that I join Barnett in his newly formed credit card department, which I accepted.

My job at Barnett was to solicit and sign up merchants who would accept the bank's new credit card, which turned out to be a "chicken or egg" scenario for the bank. If someone had a bank credit card but nowhere to use it, the card was worthless. If merchants *were* willing to take the card but no one had it, it was also worthless. In order for the credit card business to be successful, individuals had to receive the credit card, *and* merchants needed to accept it as a form of payment, almost at the same time.

Recognizing this, Barnett Bank purchased several hundred thousand names from the local credit bureau. This list naturally contained errors and mistakes, including the names of deceased people, but Barnett accounted for this in its projections. Using this list, the bank organized and executed a "drop" and sent out unsolicited, but valid, credit cards with $300 or $500 credit limits to approximately 300,000 individuals from the list who lived in Central Florida.

This opportunity put me at the forefront of the credit card business as it first emerged in the area. With the 300,000 credit cards in people's hands, the "customer" or "user" part of the equation had been solved. Now with people carrying Barnett's credit card, the bank then needed merchants to accept the cards, which is where my main duties lay. As part of my job, I delivered presentations to groups of 50 to 100 business owners, such as folks who were in the restaurant business, and convinced them to accept the bank's credit card as payment. I wore my gold-colored sports jacket with a BankAmericard logo on the pocket and walked up and down Park Avenue and all over Central Florida, knocking on the doors of different businesses, explaining the benefits of accepting the bank credit cards, and guiding them through paperwork to join the program. I learned then that no matter the way you sell, the process boils down to one main objective: Convince the audience that you have something that will benefit them. You can sell all day long, but ultimately, the customer has to buy.

Over the next two years, I signed up approximately 1,400 merchants. In retrospect, I likened it to "shooting ducks in a pond." Once a merchant agreed to accept the credit card, they would often close their accounts with other banks and form a relationship with Barnett instead, wanting to keep their credit card and cash deposits at the same institution. Getting my foot in the door was the hard part, but once I established a relationship, the customer and I both benefited. In comparison, the approximately 30 officers of the bank, who had other duties, were also supposed to sign merchants as part of their job. However, many were not comfortable as "salesmen" and, therefore, only produced about 250 merchant sign-ups in total.

And because I was performing at such a high level of success, I was invited to participate in the officer meetings, even though I was just a college student at the time. I was in the right place at the right time, doing the right kind of work.

Impressed by my results, Otto Souder, then the head of the bank's marketing department, said, "Well, if you're out knocking on doors and talking to prospective businesses about accepting our bank credit card, we would like for you to pitch all of the bank's services while you're at it."

With his recommendation, I transferred from the credit card department to the business development department, which was part of marketing. One of my jobs involved calling on businesses that had large accounts at the bank, making sure they were happy. After understanding how customers could benefit from the bank's different services, I became passionate about my work and succeeded in bringing new business to the bank.

The Peter Principle, a 1969 book and principle developed by Laurence J. Peter, states that a person who is competent at their job will earn a promotion, but if they lack the skills needed for the higher role, they will be incompetent at the new level and will not be promoted again. However, if the person *is* competent in the new role, they will continue to be promoted until reaching a level at which they are incompetent. In essence, if you rise above your level of competence, you will be pulled up to the next rank. And I was fortunate enough to be pulled up.

In my fifth and final year at Rollins, Charlie Rice received an offer to become the president of Barnett Bank's holding company in Jacksonville, Florida, and he took Otto Souder with him to lead statewide marketing initiatives there. With Otto gone, a large gap was left in the local Barnett Bank's marketing department. At the age of 21, I was promoted to fill that role, and when I graduated from Rollins in 1971 with my MBA, I accepted the full-time position running the marketing and business development departments for all five Barnett Banks in the Orlando area.

In comparison to marketing, the business development side of banking is more of a salesman's job, as it primarily revolves around promoting the bank's services, seeking new customers, and providing service to existing customers. The sales strategies involved in banking were distinctly unique, considering the market for the services was so broad. As long as someone was not already a customer, they were a prospect. My duties included approaching many diverse businesses, presenting the bank's offerings, and creating valuable relationships with prospective account holders and prospective customers.

Being successful meant that I also had a lot of fun. I consider myself lucky to have been in that position, especially at such a young age, since that is how I got my foot in the door and began building my Rolodex of relationships.

When Charlie Rice left for Jacksonville, the bank elected a new president by the name of J. Blair Culpepper. Blair achieved his position through an untraditional route. Instead of coming up through commercial lending like most bank presidents, his expertise was in marketing and business development. I think this is why we became close—because I did what he used to do. Blair would take me to events, openings, and other gatherings and introduce me to people, or if he could not attend, he would ask me to go in his place. At an early age, I would independently attend events meant for senior banking executives and officers, meeting new people and introducing myself. A certain level of confidence and assertiveness was required, but I never felt as if I had a disadvantage because of my age.

If 100 people gathered in a room, 80 of them would almost always be over the age of 50. In these crowds, I stuck out—a desirable starting position for any salesman. With that advantage, I approached everyone that I could, gauging interest in our banking services without being too overbearing and walking away from conversations with people remembering my name.

There is no question that the greatest lesson learned from my time at the bank had nothing to do with finance or credit. Rather, what I learned about relationships carried throughout the rest of my career. I met hundreds of people while at Barnett Bank, and over time, I established a reputation as an outgoing individual who was very involved in the community. As part of this effort, I gained access to a large network of people.

CHAPTER 4
THE WINTER PARK JAYCEES

"The skills I learned allowed me to stand before large audiences with confidence, which taught me to build and nurture relationships that would define my life moving forward."

I joined the Winter Park Jaycees in 1967 after first hearing about the organization from a Colonial High School coach. I never had him as a coach, but one day, I happened to meet him at a local sub shop. While having lunch and listening to his description of the Jaycees, I was intrigued and decided to attend my first meeting.

The Jaycees, originally founded as the US Junior Chamber of Commerce, was an organization of young professionals that taught leadership development through community service. A national organization with hundreds of chapters, the Jaycees established a Winter Park chapter about 15 years before I joined. At one point, the Winter Park chapter had 140 members who would meet every week at seven o'clock in the morning. If a member had a community project in the works or headed a committee, the expectation was that they would make a presentation in front of the entire organization and divide duties among volunteers, in an effort to undertake community service events and teach members valuable leadership experiences. A member had to be between the ages of 18 and 35, which meant they were the prime audience to benefit from these leadership opportunities. Once a member reached 35 years old, they would leave the club and become an "exhausted rooster" upon retiring from the organization.

I actually joined the Winter Park chapter a little before my 18th birthday, during my first year at Rollins, and I had the opportunity to be a part of several impactful community projects. In one instance, other members and I helped a friend run as the president of the national Jaycees organization. We campaigned across the country, visiting many chapters and organizing events for his candidacy. At the time, the Orlando Jaycees chapter was the largest chapter in the nation with more than 1,000 members. Thinking of ways to deal with their large size and voting power, members of the Winter Park Jaycees visited other small communities in Florida with chapters, such as Kissimmee and Apopka, and teamed up with them. With their combined membership, we could ultimately outvote the Orlando Jaycees, which provided an important lesson about the distribution of political power and how to unify a group of people around a common objective.

Jaycees chapters undertook a significant number of community projects, ranging from 15 to 20 per year, and during my time as a member, I was involved in multiple projects and made many connections and lifelong friendships. I was a part of the Jaycees for more than 10 years, and the experience was fun, rewarding, and very social. I established a camaraderie with many fellow Jaycees who ultimately re-entered my life as lawyers, architects, or other professionals once I began my career. The men in the Jaycees were there to learn how to take charge, present ideas, and be successful in community engagement using their leadership talents, not to personally profit. The Jaycees attracted dynamic, motivated, and energetic individuals who wanted to learn and grow with the byproduct being that, along the way, they did good for the community.

Today, my involvement with the Winter Park Jaycees is one of the first entries on my resume, as I credit my ability to build connections to this organization. At that time, very few programs existed for teaching young men how to put two sentences together and convince their audiences of a "call to action." The skills I learned allowed me to stand before large audiences with confidence, which taught me to build and nurture relationships that would define my life moving forward.

One very important relationship was with my future business partner, Larry Godwin. Although we originally met while working at Barnett Bank, we really became close friends while being a part of the Jaycees. From there, we secured our real estate licenses together, started The Keewin Real Property Company, and completed innumerable deals as partners.

All of this despite the fact that when my time came to become the president of the Winter Park Jaycees chapter in 1969, Larry approached me and said, "Hey, I'm older than you. I should be the next president." Even though I had been a member of the organization for about a year longer than he had.

I agreed, allowing him to serve in 1969, and I assumed that role in 1970.

With the president before Larry being Bob Koch, a close friend today, and the president after me being Mason Blake, who also remains a good friend, these strong relationships paid off in spades over the years. Therefore, I was happy to accommodate Larry—even if it meant waiting on the Jaycees presidency for a year.

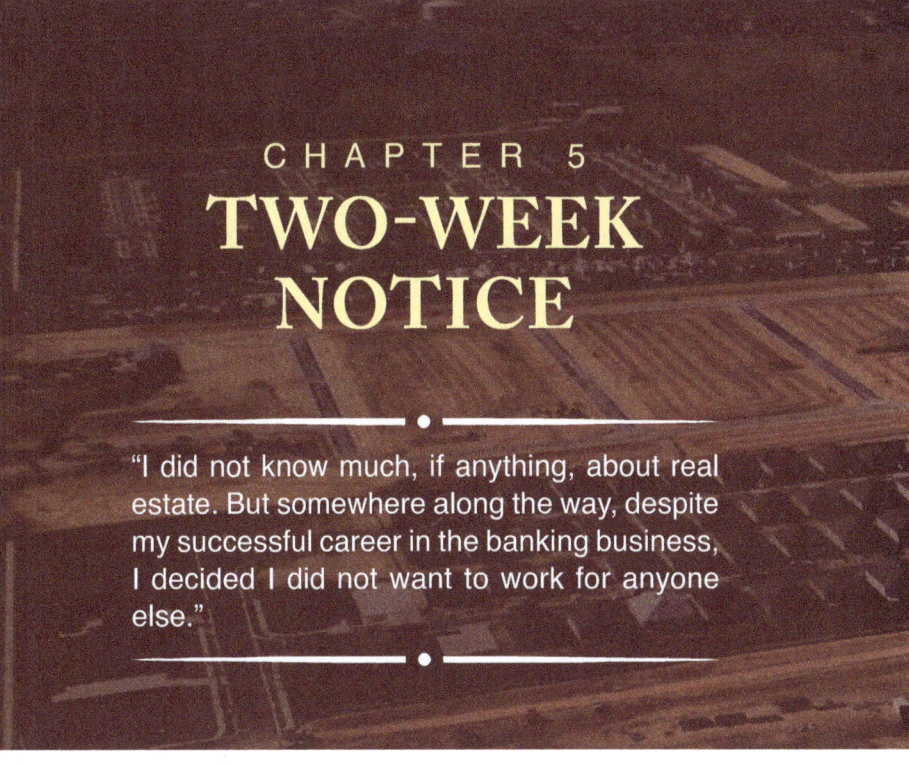

CHAPTER 5
TWO-WEEK NOTICE

"I did not know much, if anything, about real estate. But somewhere along the way, despite my successful career in the banking business, I decided I did not want to work for anyone else."

Most of our bank officers preferred to spend their early mornings in the company breakroom, sipping free coffee, but Larry Godwin and I always walked to the drug store next door, paying for our coffee and meeting on our own. I guess we were a bit contrarian.

Toward the end of 1973, a Winter-Park-based community bank approached Larry with a job offer. While he did consider it, he ultimately realized that he would not want to compete directly with Barnett Bank in the same town and declined the position. That community bank kept after him and eventually revised the offer: Larry could work at their bank in South Orlando, outside of the Winter Park market. I had a definite opinion on the matter. Since it was such a good opportunity, I told Larry that if he did not take it, he "would not be my friend anymore." The intention was always that Larry would work at this community bank for a few years before joining me full-time at the real estate company we would start together—a plan concocted after years of early-morning coffee at that next-door drug store.

Two years prior, on October 1, 1971, Walt Disney World opened in Orlando. The real estate market experienced historic, unprecedented growth, presenting opportunities to just about anyone with a real estate license. Many people entered the real estate business with minimal experience yet exited deals with large profits. In some instances, people turned a profit by buying and selling property to other speculators, which was highly unusual. Typically, a speculator would buy a property, hold on to it for several years, and then sell it to a high-paying user, not to another speculator. Real estate began exchanging hands two or three times in short periods of time, making undeveloped land an exciting sector within the market.

I did not know much, if anything, about real estate. But somewhere along the way, despite my successful career in the banking business, I decided I did not want to work for anyone else, even though I had a great job and an excellent relationship with my boss. The way I saw it, I had formed hundreds of valuable relationships with folks from Rollins and also in the community. I could enter the investment real estate business, which would entail dealing with the relationships that I had built over those years, encouraging them to invest in real estate deals, raising investment capital, and forming partnerships. I often joke that a common misnomer helped: People thought if someone had worked for a bank, they were smart. Not necessarily true, but that perception certainly helped me get my foot in the door.

Being ambitious, Larry and I decided that we would quit the bank, and we would quit at the same time. On December

15, 1973, we flipped a coin to determine which one of us would tell Blair Culpepper about our decision to leave the bank.

I have always been lucky when it comes to games of chance, but on that day, I lost the coin toss. On Saturday morning, I called Blair, which was a bit unusual as it was the weekend.

"What's up?" he said, answering the phone.

"Hello, Blair, how are you today? I just wanted to see if Larry and I could come talk to you."

"Well, what do you want?" Blair asked. His tone was a bit more serious.

"Just to talk, if you have a few minutes," I responded, to which he repeated his prior question.

With me hemming and hawing, his next statement was, "You're going to quit, aren't you?" Before I could respond, he continued, "I'll see you at seven o'clock Monday morning," and hung up the phone.

I sat there on the other end of the line, blown away and scared to death. Aside from my job at the Rollins library as a student, the bank was the only job I'd ever had. For the rest of the weekend, I dreaded what he would say to me on Monday, not knowing how this would go as I had never quit a job before. Also, I only had about $4,000 in my bank account, so I did not have a large cash cushion. It's not like I was leaving for a big salary ... or any salary at all.

Come Monday morning at 7 a.m., I closed the door to Blair's office behind me, took a seat at his desk, and listened as he vehemently tried to talk me out of this decision. He opined that I was making a mistake and giving up a rare chance at a great career. The economy was degrading, with 1974 marking the beginning of one of the toughest recessions in US history. People would soon begin losing their jobs, and business opportunities would become scarce. In other words, it was probably the worst time I could have picked for a career change, leaving the comfort and security (and salary) of the bank. I was 21 years old with a bank car, an office on Park Avenue, and an unlimited expense account. I had earned all of that through my performance, but in a lot of ways, I was very fortunate that people like Blair Culpepper and Charlie Rice had provided me with those opportunities. Many others in their position would not have, with me being so young.

Despite the risk and Blair's fervent warning, I still put in my two-week notice.

Then, as if having this conversation with Blair was not difficult enough, Charlie Rice called me very shortly after I stepped back into my office.

"What in the hell are you doing?" he asked. "And why are you doing it?"

"I don't know why I'm doing it," I replied. "I just want to take the opportunity to work for myself."

"Is there anything I can do at all to convince you to stay?"

"No, sir, there isn't."

Charlie sighed. "Well, if that's the case, you have my word that if anything happens and you need to come back to the bank, you will always have a job waiting for you anytime."

His promise strengthened the backbone I needed to leave with confidence. And after December 15, 1973—over 50 years ago—I never received another W-2 paycheck.

CHAPTER 6
REAL ESTATE LICENSE

"When you are motivated and believe in yourself, you cannot imagine a situation where you make a decision and do not succeed, or else you would never take the chance in the first place."

Anticipating that we were going to leave our jobs at Barnett, in the fall of 1973, Larry and I decided to obtain our real estate licenses, prior to our departure. In Florida then, and certainly now, several private companies offered sanctioned preparatory courses for those interested in taking the Florida real estate license exam. These courses were not a requirement for securing a license; they simply coached participants on how to take the test and provided background knowledge to anyone learning from scratch. Or so I thought.

As I applied for my real estate license, I decided to forgo this 10-week prep course, instead believing I was smart enough to ace the test without any external help. On that scheduled day, I went to the testing site and answered the questions in a logical way. I left the building feeling as if I had made a near-perfect score, but when I received my results in the mail... I had *failed*.

Turns out, these preparatory courses taught more than basic fundamentals. While I had "logically" answered questions, the prep course would have trained me to answer them differently, even providing some word-for-word answers. For example, one question asked, "When is a deed effective?" According to the law, a deed is effective when it is *delivered* and *recorded*, so if a multiple-choice answer did not contain *both* the words "delivered" and "recorded," I did not choose it. However, if I had taken the preparatory course, the instructor would have told me the correct answer would only need to contain one of those words. Without knowing the tricks of the test, I responded to each exam question with what I believed to be a rational answer, not according to how the test was prepared.

Here I was, about to quit my job at the bank, and I could not take the next preparatory course for another two months. As a result, I left the bank and entered the real estate business without a license, and for the first few months of my new career, I was not able to legally receive a real estate commission if I earned one. However, I continued forward despite this temporary setback. After taking the prep course several months later and understanding the correct answers, I scored a 98 on the final exam and received my real estate license.

When I entered the real estate industry in January of 1974, the uncertainty was palpable. Blair Culpepper had predicted the future when he warned me about the approaching recession. At the time, I had too much energy and ambition to worry that any economic downturn would matter. As it turned out, this decline worked in my favor: Unwittingly, I had entered the industry at one of the best buying opportunities in US history for speculating on undeveloped or vacant property. I chose to make my first investment in raw land (though this focus would change in 1978). Because of the weak market conditions, I could buy land cheaper than what it would be worth two to five years later, with terms that normally would not have been offered. While I will not say I foresaw this ahead of time, I did recognize that once I purchased a parcel of property, I had no expectation of selling it right away. I knew that we would hold on to the property for at least three to five years. The timing felt right for implementing this strategy, so I began looking to join a local company that invested in or syndicated undeveloped real estate.

I left my position at Barnett Bank on January 1, 1974, and went to work for a real estate investment company called Odyssey, Inc., which had been actively connecting investors with land opportunities for the past seven years. The company had created a solid reputation for itself, having been active during what I refer to as Orlando's "heyday" in the early Disney years, and I already had personal relationships with several people there. Eager to learn more from experienced, established professionals in the field, I joined the company with three intentions: to raise capital, build partnerships, and make money.

In hindsight, entering the real estate industry during a recession was probably one of those risky moves I made only because I was too young and self-assured to even consider the possibility of failure. However, many times, it is these decisions that make the biggest difference in one's life, for when you are motivated and believe in yourself, you cannot imagine a situation where you make a decision and do not succeed, or else you would never take the chance in the first place. Therefore, you end up with the belief that, one way or another, you will make it work. I never thought for a moment that I would not make it, even if I did not fully know *how* I would. Instead, I pushed forward with putting deals together because I knew, if nothing else, I could do that. I also knew that as long as I could find a piece of property with the right investment characteristics, I had enough relationships and knew enough people to raise the money to make that investment.

I closed my first deal in June of 1974, six months after I left the bank. This first parcel of land was purchased for several reasons, the first of which was that the property, located between Orlando and Apopka, sat on US 441, a major road that runs through the middle of Orlando. The 37.5-acre tract had been almost bisected by that road years ago and had nearly 3,000 feet of frontage on both sides of US 441. Such a large amount of frontage and exposure not only increased its value but also meant that I could divide the land into separate parcels, and each new parcel would have major road frontage. The second reason I wanted to purchase the land was because it was close to a "proposed" road to be built that would connect Interstate 4 (I-4) to US 441, which would have a potentially dramatic impact on the value of the land around this new connector at US 441, i.e., the Maitland Boulevard Extension.

Finally, the last characteristic that attracted me to the property was the existing building on the parcel of land next to it: Citrus Central. After freezes in the 1980s, most orange trees in the Orlando area died, causing a majority of the citrus industry to relocate 150 miles south near Lake Okeechobee. However, back then, Orlando was a major area for orange production, reflected in the name Orange County. Citrus Central was a

20,000-square-foot office building that served as the marketing arm for the Florida citrus industry. This adjacent property was also zoned as I-2 (industrial), whereas the property I purchased was zoned as A-1 (agricultural), which I saw as an important opportunity to create value. As long as my property remained agricultural, the land could only be used to grow oranges, but I saw the potential here.

If I could rezone the property to industrial, rather than agricultural, many different businesses could purchase pieces of the land for their company facilities, which would create a much wider range of potential buyers and at a significantly higher land value. In addition, the tax laws at the time encouraged folks to invest in the citrus business. When purchasing the citrus land, we would assign a value to the trees (separate from the land value) and receive an investment tax credit on that amount, as well as tax deductions for the depreciation of the tree value. Due to these different tax benefits, the investors in this first deal would, and did, receive a nice return on their investment within the first year based on the tax attributes. Using all of these facts in my presentation, I raised $50,000 by having 10 individuals each invest $5,000, formed an investment partnership, and purchased the property. In addition to the cash down payment of $50,000, the sellers of the land extended a private purchase-money mortgage of $400,000 to complete the full purchase price.

Although this first purchase resulted in a successful return to the investors, I still learned a valuable lesson. If I had decided to buy the land only because of the advantage I identified (a new road from I-4 to US 441), this would have been a big mistake. At the time of this investment, we "knew" the road *would* be built, but we did not exactly know *when*. The investors and I made the purchase in 1974, and although I expected this new road to be built in 1977, the road did not come to fruition until 1985. Therefore, if we had bought this property solely on the basis of that road, we would have had to wait for more than a decade to see any profit. Fortunately, the amount of road frontage and exposure turned out to be a significant asset, and we were successful.

I still have the brochure that I made and presented to prospective investors. Within it is a large map of the proposed new road, a dubious selling point as it turned out, yet the one I chose to feature. Since then, I have never again bought real estate because of the *potential* or *promise* of a new road. Rather, I first verify the actual timing on construction.

For putting this deal together, I received a 5 percent ownership interest as the general partner, and I earned two commissions, one upon buying the property and the other when selling it. When we closed on the acquisition, my commission was $26,833; however, the seller chose to only pay me $16,833 upfront and deferred payments of $5,000 per year for the subsequent two years. Holding a check for $16,833 in my hand—the amount of my full annual salary at the bank—felt like I had hit the jackpot . . . and with my very first deal in less than six months. My career in real estate had started.

The $16,833 Check in 1974

However, as each month passed, the $16,833 began to be used up, for unlike my regularly salaried job, real estate does not have weekly paychecks. I watched as, month by month, the $16,833 dwindled to $15,000, then $14,000, and then $13,000—all while, as Blair Culpepper had warned, the economy worsened. Although Odyssey, Inc. had been in its prime during early Disney times, almost every employee and associate, minus the company's founder and myself, left during my first year at the firm. If not for those two deferred payments of $5,000 in 1975 and 1976, I may have had to take Charlie Rice up on his offer and return to the bank.

During this time, I also began participating in politics, an activity that I have remained involved in throughout my career. Bob Hattaway, a friend of mine who had been president of the Florida Jaycees and then the national vice president of the US Jaycees, knew I had helped a friend run for national Jaycees president. Therefore, when he decided to run for a seat in the Florida House of Representatives, he asked me to serve as his campaign manager. My role would be to oversee everything, from raising money to advertising to organizing volunteers, and somehow, despite my lack of experience, I became engaged in the process. I am grateful I did, for one of the attributes I have always carried with me is normally saying "yes" to opportunities and challenges, even ones that I'm not sure of. These opportunities most often lead to success as well as great relationships and experiences. In the case of running Bob's campaign, it led to all three.

After a successful campaign, Bob was elected to the Florida House of Representatives, where he served from 1974 to 1982, and I joined his family's real estate company, Altamonte Realty, to continue the work I started at Odyssey, Inc.—creating partnerships and purchasing investment real estate. However, it was around this time that two major opportunities changed both my career and life in more consequential ways than I ever expected.

CHAPTER 7

OPPORTUNITY ONE—EURO CAPITAL PARTNERS

"I did not do anything exceptionally remarkable to enter such a transformative era of my life. . . . The people I met and the relationships I established paved the way for my future—without me realizing it at the time."

For decades, Apopka, the second-largest city in Orange County, has been known as the "foliage capital of the world." The history of the city and its connections to flora extends back to the early 1800s when farmers grew vegetable gardens, cotton, corn, sugar cane, and later, orange groves, but it was in the 1920s when growing ferns became so popular that Apopka earned the nickname "The Fern City." Seeing how ferns prospered in this environment, people began raising other types of ornamental plants, turning Apopka into the green town it is today.[1]

In the 1970s, the city's reputation made it a prime location for the construction of greenhouses, the vast majority of which used fiberglass at the time. While fiberglass continues to be the most common option, true and lasting "greenhouses," as found in Europe—particularly Holland—are made from real glass, i.e., glasshouses. Constructed from high-quality, durable materials, these glass greenhouses can last for over a hundred years. Today, driving along the back roads of Apopka, you can see hundreds of gardens, plant nurseries, and greenhouses, some of which have been around for decades, in the yards of homes and businesses alike.

In 1977, Van der Hoeven, one of the largest glass greenhouse fabricators and sellers in Holland, wished to branch out to US markets. Naturally, the company chose Apopka for its US headquarters due to the climate of the region and its botany-centered culture, with the intention of expanding into surrounding regions and states over time. Representatives for the Van der Hoeven company saw the "for sale" sign in front of the 37.5 acres I purchased in 1974 (the partnership was named Golden Grove of Florida, Ltd.) and immediately expressed interest, proceeding to purchase 7.5 acres of the land. US 441 divided the original 37.5 acres into two parcels—30 acres on one side and 7.5 acres on the other—each offering excellent frontage and exposure.

Apart from making this land sale, I never imagined my relationship with Van der Hoeven would lead to much more than this one simple transaction, but in September of the same year, the New York lawyer representing Van der Hoeven called me. Also being of Dutch heritage, he explained that he only served Dutch clients who were looking to invest in American real estate, and his current clients, a father and son, had sold their dairy business in the Netherlands. Although they had already invested in farmland in Arkansas, they wanted to expand into traditional real estate by investing several million dollars in Florida, where they had been attracted by Disney.

"Would you like to meet them?" the attorney asked. Thinking this could be another great opportunity to pursue, I agreed, and the lawyer scheduled a breakfast meeting for January 30, 1978, almost four months in advance. Up to that point, I had never arranged a meeting that far out.

I did not hear another word from anyone for all of those months, but I arrived on time at the Quality Inn High Q Hotel in Orlando at eight o'clock in the morning on January 30. There, I met the gentleman, Ed Leerdam, and his father. After talking for a short while, we immediately hit it off. Ed wanted to move to the US and open a real estate business that would cater to successful Dutch businesspeople like him who had sold their businesses for large sums and wished to diversify their assets via real estate investment opportunities in America.

At this point, after four years in the business, I had enough knowledge and experience bringing investors together and forming limited partnerships as a real estate syndicator to answer his questions and act as the needed resource for him. Likewise, Ed provided an exciting pool of potential investors, all of whom had very different types of successful companies in Holland and related to Ed's business background. Some of these entrepreneurs owned grocery store chains, butcher shops, Coca-Cola distributors, and brewing companies, one of which was Grolsch Brewery, a legendary Dutch beer company dating back to the 1600s. With this impressive investor list to work with, I would no longer have to go "knocking on doors" to find potential investors. Instead, Ed and I could seek larger real estate deals with this dedicated source of capital. Seeing that I could bring my expertise and Ed could bring the capital, a potentially lucrative partnership began to take shape from this first meeting.

Within a few months, I flew to The Hague, the third-largest city in the Netherlands, and met him again. We started a business together at the end of 1978, intending to initially operate in Central Florida, although we did look at properties in other cities at times, such as Columbia, South Carolina, and Paducah, Kentucky. We also established an office in The Hague, and with an administrative partner there, Ed and I would visit the Netherlands four or five times a year. Similarly, groups of Dutch business folks would fly to Florida a few times a year to review potential investment properties we intended to acquire.

In 1980, we formed the new company originally called Euro American Investors Group but later changed its name to Euro Capital Partners. We operated during an exciting time, and over these years, I was fortunate enough to see the lives and families of business associates and friends grow alongside my own. One investor, in particular, had sold his family grocery business to a conglomerate, and we established and continued a business and personal relationship for over a decade. When I first met this investor, his youngest daughter was nine years old, but after 12 years of business, she had turned 21.

On reflection, I recognize that I did not do anything exceptionally remarkable to enter such a transformative era of my life. In my eyes, I had simply sold a piece of land for a profit, yet doing so opened the door to this Dutch attorney, which then led to that important meeting with Ed and his father. Everything fell into place, and the people I met and the relationships I established paved the way for my future—without me realizing it at the time.

CHAPTER 8
OPPORTUNITY TWO—UNIVERSAL STUDIOS

> "Little did I know, this friendship established in graduate school . . . would not only be a cherished, pivotal professional accomplishment and business opportunity but also place me at the center of one of the biggest economic development deals in Central Florida's history."

Around the same time that Ed and I established Euro Capital Partners, a second opportunity dramatically impacted my career and future, becoming one of my proudest business accomplishments. And this opportunity all began with a phone call from a former Crummer classmate, Bill Bieberbach, in 1977.

The class sizes were small for undergraduate courses at Rollins, and the same was true for the MBA classes at the Crummer School, which meant that you couldn't "run and hide" during lectures or group assignments. In classes with only 10 or so students and 1 professor, everyone had to speak up and participate. I became close friends with many people in my MBA cohort due to this, Bill included, despite our four-year age gap. We were part of the same study group, and on numerous occasions, our group would go to Bill's apartment on campus for late-night study sessions.

Bill served in the Navy for four years prior to starting at Rollins, where he became a resident advisor (RA) in one of the dorms. After graduating at the same time as I did, Bill worked for Walt Disney World for several years, and afterward, he secured a job with Taft Entertainment, the theme park subsidiary of Taft Broadcasting Company, a Cincinnati media conglomerate that owned and managed a number of TV and radio stations. Taft Entertainment operated in what was called the "hard ride" theme park business, referring to roller coasters, Ferris wheels, and other amusement park rides. As such, this subsidiary owned Kings Dominion theme park in Virginia, Carowinds in North Carolina, Marineland in California, and Kings Island in Ohio, one of the oldest theme parks in America.

Bill Bieberbach was, and still is, one of my closest friends. When I picked up the phone that day, we exchanged greetings, and he told me, "You're going to get a call from a guy named Nelson Schwab, the head of Taft Entertainment, our theme park subsidiary."

The yellow legal pad page where I jotted down Nelson Schwab's contact information now sits in a glass frame in my office. The page has Schwab's name (with the note "trip down" beside it), his phone number, and the location of a 100-acre parcel of land in the middle of Disney (or the "womb of Disney," as we would later call it) that Taft Entertainment hoped to purchase.

The bottom left-hand corner of the page is ripped from where I tore it off the legal pad and stored it away for future reference.

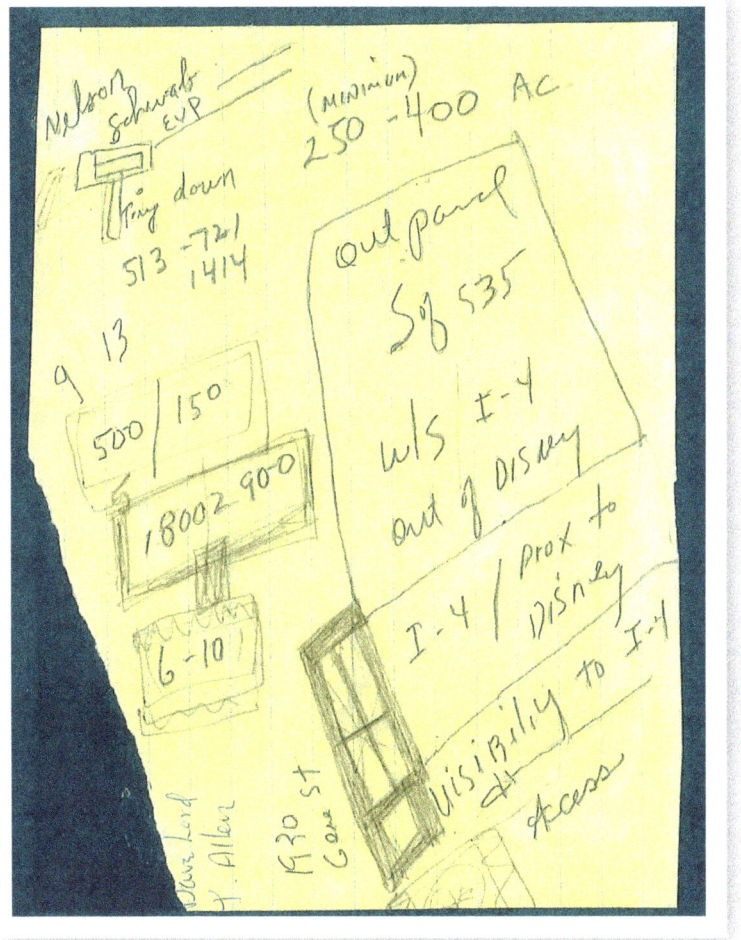

The Torn Paper with Nelson Schwab's Contact Information

It was not too long after my talk with Bill that I called Schwab, whereby he provided me with more details: Taft Entertainment was interested in building a "hard ride" theme park in Central Florida, and Schwab and his "associates" wanted to visit Orlando and tour some potential sites. Their only criteria: This property had to be immediately adjacent to and front on I-4. Schwab and his "associates" scheduled an Orlando visit, and I had a month and a half to prepare a list of potential locations and coordinate a personal tour with them.

The conversation with Schwab clued me in to the sensitivity required for this project. He was not forthright with many details, which made me think the project was larger and more significant than he originally suggested. Realizing that I could not disclose any of the details to anyone, I asked Linda, my wife, to undertake the research of potential properties necessary for this meeting. She researched every intersection along I-4 from Lake Mary, north of Orlando, all the way to US 27, which is in Polk County. About 30 parcels of land were appropriate fits, so using plat maps and aerial photographs for each parcel, we identified the names of all of these property owners and property information.

When Schwab and two other gentlemen arrived in Orlando (whom he identified only as "investors") a month after our first call, I rented a helicopter to fly them from Lake Mary to Lakeland, guiding them over each parcel of land with maps and well-researched property descriptions. Earlier that day, Schwab had introduced the investors only as "Jay" and "Al." The first "investor," Jay, had slicked-back, jet-black hair with small, round glasses, and the second, Al, looked like Kojak: a large guy with a shaved head and the biggest gold Rolex on his wrist that I'd ever seen. Interesting characters, I could tell.

After the property tour, Schwab, his "investors," and I sat down for dinner at La Belle Verriere (translated to English,

"The Beautiful Glass"), a Park Avenue French restaurant in a building that was owned by the Charles Hosmer Morse Foundation, known for having the largest collection of Louis Comfort Tiffany stained glass in the world. Priceless pieces of stained glass backlit the restaurant, transforming the space into a small art gallery. Once our food arrived, I began promoting Orlando and encouraging them to choose Central Florida for their new business venture, unsure if they had already decided on a location for this theme park. I launched into a story about Florida Governor Bob Graham, who later became our US senator. As governor, he had been flying out to California every few months, meeting with Hollywood studio executives and trying to get them to "make movies" in Florida.

"Our governor has been to Hollywood numerous times and met with Lew Wasserman, among others," I told them. "I even read a small story in the *Orlando Sentinel* rumor column, Hushpuppies, that a working motion studio may be coming here, and *not just to make movies*."

As soon as I mentioned this "rumor," the energy around the three men suddenly shifted, becoming very tense, whereas before it had been friendly and conversational. The man with the slicked-back hair, Jay, reached across the table and pointed his finger to my nose, almost touching it. My eyes were wide.

"What do you know about this?" he asked in a stern voice. "What *exactly* did you read? I want to know immediately."

Scared to death, I blubbered out a reply, promising I would find the newspaper article, to which he replied, "This is one of the most important things you're ever going to do—finding out what that newspaper said."

The fact that I had struck a very sensitive nerve was evident, so I did two things: One, I looked for the Hushpuppies article, though I never found it after hours of searching. Two, I answered a phone call from Bill Bieberbach, who asked, "How was your meeting with Universal Studios?"

The missing piece of the puzzle clicked into place. Bells went off. I must have been talking to officials from *Universal Studios* in conjunction with Taft Entertainment. This meant, as it turned out, that *Universal Studios was interested in building a theme park in Orlando to compete with Walt Disney World*—a venture that would be monumental for the local and state economy and a historic opportunity for every person involved, should it happen.

Universal Studios was part of MCA Inc. (formally named the Music Corporation of America), which was founded in 1924 by Jules Stein as a Chicago-based agency that booked performers for clubs and dance halls. Though Stein found success, MCA only began expanding into the billion-dollar empire that it is today under the leadership of Lew Wasserman, a businessman, talent agent, and Hollywood legend described by *The New York Times* as "arguably the most powerful and influential Hollywood titan in the four decades after World War II."[1] Therefore, when Wasserman and MCA executives decided to open a movie studio and a related theme park, they saw the success and established market of Disney and began dreaming of Orlando as the promising location. Because the industry was so competitive, MCA did not want to announce its plans and wished to keep a low profile, so they employed a third party, Taft Entertainment, to be their "stalking horse."

After talking to Bill and doing a bit of research into the history of Universal Studios, I also looked up the names of the two "investors" Schwab brought with him to the meeting and dinner. The man he introduced as Jay ended up being the CEO of MCA Recreation Services Group and the godfather and founder of Universal Studios Florida, Jay Stein. The man with the shaved head and Rolex was Albert A. Dorskind, the president of MCA Development, the company's real estate arm. Under Lew Wasserman, they were the two top dogs, directly under him as CEO.

Once again in my career, I ended up in the right place at the right time with the right relationships. Because of Bill's recommendation, Taft Entertainment and Universal Studios did not choose to interview 10 people, 4 people, or even 2 people for the job as their exclusive real estate broker. The way Schwab presented the deal to me was: "If Bill says you're the guy, you're the guy."

Little did I know, this friendship established in graduate school—a relationship Bill and I still share today, as I recently attended his 80th birthday dinner—would not only be a cherished, pivotal professional accomplishment and business opportunity but also place me at the center of one of the biggest economic development deals in Central Florida's history. During this time, Linda and I became very close not only to Jay Stein but also to a few of his close associates, particularly Barry Upton, Alan Eberly, and Steve Lew. As Universal moved toward its grand opening, these folks were instrumental in realizing what is now the landmark Universal Studios Florida in Orlando.

CHAPTER 9
THE KEEWIN REAL PROPERTY COMPANY

"Upon the official establishment of Keewin, I became the exclusive real estate broker for Universal Studios Florida, a relationship that lasted for 20 years."

A year after receiving my real estate license, I sought my broker's license, primarily due to my interest in owning an independent real estate company and thereby controlling the commission potential. Two new major real estate opportunities propelled me: Euro Capital Partners and Universal Studios Florida. In anticipation of the profound impact these projects would have on our futures, my business partner, Larry Godwin, and I founded our own real estate company. To establish the company's name, we decided to somehow combine our last names. We considered several possibilities: Godkee, Keegod, Winkee, etc., but none sounded quite as right as Keewin.

The Keewin Real Property Company (originally called The Keewin Company) was established in November 1978. More than 45 years later, I still have the same phone number that I had when we started. Our first office, located in a former two-bedroom apartment, sat above a retail store and had an open-air balcony that overlooked Park Avenue, the main shopping area in downtown Winter Park with a unique brick street, shops, cafes, and restaurants on one side and Central Park on the other.

Earlier, Larry and I had determined that if we both continued to work for a bank, we couldn't help each other, and if we both worked in the real estate business, we couldn't help each other either. Hence, Larry decided to stay involved in banking for a while, and I would manage the real estate side until Larry came to work for Keewin full-time in 1981. This is why, with Ed Leerdam moving from Holland to the US during this time, he (rather than Larry) took one available office space, and I took the other.

The only drawback was that these new offices were not yet finished. The cabinets had been ripped from the walls, and the floor had no carpet. Our first course of action was to paint and patch the walls, put in carpet, and purchase furniture. At this time, I had a friend, Mac Davidson, in the outdoor billboard business. I cannot remember why I decided to split my office with Mac at the time, other than that he was a close friend, but for the first year or so after starting Keewin, we shared that space. Mac had found unique wrought iron table legs and set out to make two "partner desks." The room was big enough where we could each have a desk with one chair behind it and two in front for clients, allowing us to work across from each other while still having our own desks. However, since I planned to open Keewin right after Thanksgiving 1978—it was well before those desks got constructed.

By necessity, my actual "first desk" was discovered when I looked through a back storage room in this former apartment building, which was filled with left-behind objects, none of which were worth much. I did not necessarily need a piece of furniture but rather anything simple to put my phone set on until I received the partner desks. Seeing an old Cutty Sark Scotch whiskey wooden crate, I retrieved it and brought it into the office. In the 20s and 30s, back before cardboard, whiskey was shipped in wooden boxes, so since this wooden crate was sturdy, I turned it on its side, pushed a director's chair in front of it, and placed my brown, push-button phone on the box. This setup remained my "first desk" for approximately two months until our formal office was completed.

The Cutty Sark Scotch Whiskey Box and Director's Chair that Served as My "First Desk"

Upon the official establishment of Keewin, I became the exclusive real estate broker for Universal Studios Florida, a relationship that lasted for 20 years. Part of my first responsibilities involved acting as the "point person" in charge of establishing the entire team for the project, recommending their civil engineer and their local attorney, and compiling a list of every vacant property for sale at each intersection between Sanford and Lakeland, an approximately 90-mile stretch.

The first piece of land in which Universal showed an interest—the address written on a yellow legal pad sheet that is still displayed in my office—proved difficult. This 100-acre property, actually located in the middle of Walt Disney World property, was owned by a man who lived in China. The geographical barrier made it impossible to contact and communicate with him, so Universal had no choice but to look elsewhere.

In addition, Universal initially wanted to have three pieces of property under contract at the same time. Executives decided they wanted options to choose from in the event that Universal's name got out to the public and the price of their prospective land skyrocketed as a result. Because of this, I tried to procure three separate properties at the same time, but unfortunately, it became unfeasible. Instead, Universal would have to take a chance on one property.

After months of intensive research, and at my recommendation, Universal gambled and proceeded to contract for one piece of land at I-4 and Kirkman Road—the location where Universal Studios Florida sits today.

The first acreage was purchased from two owners: 312.5 acres from Major Realty Corporation (at $14,400 per acre) and 111.5 acres from a subsidiary of Gulf Oil Corporation (at $71,750 per acre), with the total purchase price being $12.5 million. Before agreeing to the contract, however, Major Realty wanted to know which company was purchasing the land, for Major owned a lot of property around these 423 acres. Major Realty executives wanted to ensure that this purchase would not negatively impact their surrounding land or, alternatively, determine if this purchase would actually improve its value. Although we told Major's lawyer all that we could due to the secrecy of the project (stating that it was a Fortune 500 company and the deal would add value to their remaining land and have a historic impact), Major Realty refused to proceed without the buyer's information.

As a few weeks passed without much progress, I had an idea of how to solve this roadblock. If Universal would disclose their involvement to a trusted third party, that person could tell Major Realty, in confidence, "Although I cannot provide you the specifics of the buyer's information or name, you should absolutely go through with the deal and proceed with the contract to sell the property. Furthermore, you would be crazy not to do so as this will turn out to be a significant transaction for your company and for the entire state of Florida."

That third party turned out to be Florida's then-governor, Bob Graham. I had met Bob Graham in 1978—a significant time in my life, for this was the same year we started Keewin and I married my wife, Linda. At that time, I had been involved with Jim Williams, the 11th Lieutenant Governor of Florida for the prior eight years, in his run for the governor's race against Bob Graham in the Democratic primary. When Graham won the primary, he asked those of us who had run Jim William's campaign to join his team since we were from the conservative part of the Democratic Party. Larry and I had dinner in Daytona Beach at Graham's invitation, and there, we agreed to join his campaign, the beginning of a valuable relationship that would lead to other opportunities in the future.

When Graham was elected governor in 1979, his name came to mind when choosing this third party that we needed to assure Major Realty of the importance of this transaction. Graham knew the board chairman of Major Realty, and he had previously visited Universal Studios in California in the interest of getting the company to make movies in Florida. If I disclosed that not only did Universal intend to make movies, but they also planned to build a pivotal tourist attraction and a working motion picture studio, a core ambition of his would be actualized beyond what he ever thought was possible.

Major Realty agreed to this suggestion and signed the contract to sell the property (and placed the contract into escrow) to the "unnamed" buyer, determining that the governor's reassurance would be the trigger needed to release the executed contract from escrow. On a Saturday, I drove to St. Petersburg, knowing Governor Graham planned to attend a campaign rally there. I entered the two-story indoor arena and walked upstairs to see the governor, surrounded by 10 or so people.

"Governor Graham, I'm Allan Keen. Could I speak with you for a moment?" I asked.

The people surrounding him continued the conversation, causing the governor to miss what I said.

"It's about Universal Studios," I added. "They want to come to Orlando, not just to make movies but to open a theme park and motion picture studio."

Governor Graham then turned his attention to me. "What?" he asked.

Excusing himself from the people who surrounded him, the governor pulled me aside and retrieved a small, spiral notebook from his pocket that he was known for keeping. When he pulled it out to speak with me, I knew I had his attention.

"Do you remember Lew Wasserman, the CEO of Universal Studios?" I asked, and he nodded. "The deal is for you to call Wasserman so that he can 'officially' tell you that Universal Studios wants to come to Orlando. Then, you must call the chairman of Major Realty's board to have the contract being held in escrow released."

The governor took notes as I spoke and agreed to the mission, stating that he would contact the appropriate people and help move the project forward. Even with his urgency, a week passed before Governor Graham could talk to Lew Wasserman and Major's chairman. As soon as that happened, the contract was released from escrow the following day. And almost simultaneously, the word got out. Every media outlet now knew that Universal Studios planned to open a world-class theme park and motion picture studio in Orlando—and on Major Realty land.

CHAPTER 10
EXCLUSIVE BROKER

> "All because Universal envisioned the monumental challenge of competing with Disney and carving out a legacy in Florida history—a future that, as we all know, came to fruition, leaving a tremendous and enduring impact on the Orlando and Florida economies."

Universal closed on the property in 1980 and began construction at a later date. However, the initial 423 acres were just the start.

As the company had decided that I would be its exclusive real estate broker, we agreed to a 3-percent commission on any purchase. And we established that I would not need to receive a commission from any seller, nor would I need to cooperate with another broker. Rather, Universal wanted my direct and exclusive involvement in accumulating all of the land for its unknown project.

Over the next five years, I acquired another 35 parcels of land, totaling about 1,400 acres. If the land cost $15,000–$30,000 per acre for the initial purchase, it now cost $100,000–$200,000 per acre after Universal's involvement became public knowledge. Despite this increase in price, my instructions were to buy all of the available land, even if it was not contiguous to other land Universal owned or even if it had no approvals in place. I often bought parcels with nothing around them, in the middle of land that Universal did not own. However, as I continued to purchase property, the pieces connected over time until Universal possessed all of the sought-after land in the immediate neighborhood.

During this exciting time of land acquisition, I encountered three particularly interesting transactions.

1. **The first purchase after the initial 423-acre acquisition involved a corner of a road that was located on the backside of Universal.**

    An elderly couple owned these five acres. Their house was rustic, very basic, and secluded, so much so that it had dirt floors and was buried so deep in a wooded area that you would not know there was a house there unless told. However, despite the humble nature of the property, the couple had no interest in selling it. We presented a sizable cash offer, but money meant nothing to them. Even when we offered to buy them a new and bigger house, the couple declined. In fact, that was the last thing they wanted—to change their lifestyle and live around anyone else.

    After much effort, the couple put us in contact with their son, who was in his 60s and in the military, and he then put us in contact with his daughter, who was in her 30s. The son and granddaughter had a greater interest in selling the property than the elderly couple, which ultimately led us to a resolution: granting the couple a life estate in the property. Universal would purchase the land for $8 million in cash and obtain ownership, but the couple would be allowed to live on the property until they passed. The couple, the son, and the granddaughter all agreed, and just as the contract provided, this couple lived in their home for the rest of their lives.

2. **The second interesting transaction involved a church, which was a little further down the same road from the elderly couple.**

    Once again, we hit a roadblock: The church had no reason or interest in selling. However, we recognized that church members held their services in an older building . . . so we offered to buy them a bigger piece of land and construct a new church facility (twice as large) about a mile away. The church agreed to this arrangement, and as soon as its congregation moved to the new location, Universal assumed ownership of the property. Although this transaction represented a substantial cost to Universal, it was an incredible value for the church, even though no money ever exchanged hands.

3. **Finally, the third interesting and most important purchase occurred at a point where all these properties came together: a golf shop.**

    Universal had strategically purchased eight acres of land with I-4 frontage for $14 million from a local ranching family, knowing that a one-acre plot separated it from the other land Universal owned. This one acre was the home of a major golf merchandising shop, Edwin Watts Golf Shop. To conduct the negotiation, I flew to Panama City, Florida, the golf company's headquarters, and met with the founder's brother, Ronnie Watts, to express Universal's interest in acquiring their property. Ultimately, we reached a similar solution to the church: Universal agreed to construct a new,

10,000-square-foot golf shop (which was double the size of their previous shop) on a new piece of land with no debt attached, in exchange for Universal taking title to the current building and land.

Looking back on these three transactions and my time representing Universal, I understand what a unique experience it was being the exclusive real estate broker for such a large and impactful company. Because of the scope of the project, money was no object for Universal, and as such, normal purchase requirements and project conditions did not apply. Parcels to be acquired did not have to be adjacent to other Universal-owned properties, be properly zoned, or have road access. And because Universal paid me directly, I had a unique bargaining chip: I could tell sellers that they did not have to worry about paying any commission, and instead, they would receive the full purchase price.

Universal was the ideal client. I was most fortunate that I did not have to compete for the chance to work for Universal or put together a presentation to showcase my expertise. Because of my relationship with my Crummer School classmate, Universal chose me, trusting that I would perform at my highest capability.

Universal had a fine-tuned strategy in place and had the right people to execute it, so it spared no cost and did not pass on any land acquisition with potential. All because Universal envisioned the monumental challenge of competing with Disney and carving out a legacy in Florida history—a future that, as we all know, came to fruition, leaving a tremendous and enduring impact on the Orlando and Florida economies.

CHAPTER 11
THE ELIZABETH MORSE GENIUS FOUNDATION

"It no longer made sense to speculate on undeveloped or raw land. In response, I adopted a new business model: If I bought land, I had to use it."

Founded in 1887, Winter Park, Florida, has the reputation of being "the oasis of Central Florida." The city is one of the most desired places to live in the state (and some would say the country) primarily due to its proximity to shops, restaurants, parks, and museums, such as the Rollins Museum of Art and the Orlando Museum of Art. Its main street, Park Avenue, is the central shopping and dining area with outdoor seating, brick streets, and decorated storefronts. An active railroad track runs through downtown Winter Park, complete with a train station that serves both Amtrak and the SunRail commuter rail, and the surrounding land features Central Park and a nine-hole golf course and country club. One end of Park Avenue is anchored by Rollins College on Lake Virginia and the other by the Charles Hosmer Morse Museum of American Art. The city's location, design, and culture all make it a quaint, unique, and unquestionably great place to live.

At the center of Winter Park is 200 acres surrounded by three lakes: Lake Virginia, Lake Mizell, and Lake Berry. This land was purchased by Chicago industrialist Charles Hosmer Morse who, in 1904, became the biggest landowner in Winter Park. The land, named the Genius Preserve, remained in the Morse family and was passed down through generations: first to Charles Morse's daughter, Elizabeth Morse Genius, and her husband, Dr. Richard M. Genius; then to Morse's granddaughter, Jeannette Genius McKean, and her husband, Hugh F. McKean, who later became the 10th president of Rollins College. Untouched for nearly 100 years, three buildings sat on the land: the historic wood-frame Ward House that was built in the late 1800s as a packing house for citrus and the Genius/Mckean Spanish-Mediterranean estate home that was named "Wind Song." As Rollins College has miles of frontage on Lake Virginia, you can stand on the campus and look across the water at the Wind Song estate where Jeannette and Rollins President McKean last lived. I was fortunate to have McKean as Rollins president for the first two years of my college career, though I never had the opportunity to attend one of his cookouts on the Wind Song property, which he would famously host for students and faculty alike.

In the 50s, 60s, and 70s, the public was allowed to drive down Genius Drive, a dirt road that ran through the Morse family property, to view the oak trees, orange groves, and peaceful scenery. The property was also home to more than 100 free-ranging peacocks, some of which would periodically wander into nearby neighborhoods and be seen as "the community's pets." And although the family's charitable foundation closed access and gated the property in 1987, this land remained integral to Winter Park.

Today, the Morse/Genius/McKean family is characterized by philanthropy. Charles Hosmer Morse funded Winter Park's first town hall on the condition that his gift remain anonymous during his lifetime. He also leased land to the city for Central Park on Park Avenue and similarly contributed to a diverse range of organizations, including the Women's Christian Temperance Union, the Woman's Club of Winter Park, and Rollins College.[1] Perhaps the most charitable decisions, however, came from the two Morse siblings. Richard M. Genius, Jr. established the Elizabeth Morse Charitable Trust and the Elizabeth Morse Genius Charitable Trust to honor his mother's memory, and Jeannette Genius McKean founded the Charles Hosmer Morse Foundation in the name of her grandfather.[2] Both organizations hold a phenomenal reputation for maintaining the beauty and culture of Winter Park, notably in areas of art and education.

Jeannette and Hugh McKean were a lively and active couple who shared a passion for art above all else. The Charles Hosmer Morse Foundation was founded out of this passion and principally supported the collection of Louis Comfort Tiffany glass. In 1942, Jeannette created the Morse Gallery of Art on the Rollins campus, and by 1955, it had held its first public exhibition. The organization then purchased the home of Louis Comfort Tiffany in Long Island, New York, after the house burned down. Only remnants of the stained glass survived, and because the glass was put together with lead, much of it melted in the fire. As the couple's collection grew and as they continued to restore hundreds of glass artworks—some of the best in the world—back to their former glory, they eventually compiled more than 4,000 pieces with an estimated value of over $6 million by the 1980s. Because the foundation bought even more glass from families and estates on top of what it had restored, it soon needed a bigger location. The foundation designed, constructed, and in 1995, opened the Charles Morse Museum of American Art in a larger, modern building on North Park Avenue, where it is still located today. All told, the museum is 42,000 square feet and displays the largest Tiffany stained glass collection in the world.[3]

Jeannette, Hugh, and the foundation were very intent on not accepting the public's money to finance the new museum's initial construction nor did they want the museum's entry fee to be too expensive. Rather, the museum would be privately financed and have an affordable cost of admission to ensure that everyone could enjoy it. With these stipulations in mind, the family had to independently fund the construction without taking key resources away from its foundations, which provided support to worthy causes in the surrounding community. Because of this need, in the late 1990s, the Charles Hosmer Morse Foundation owned the 200 acres at the center of Winter Park entitled through the local government, with the intention of selling 160 acres of this strategic land for a unique and special residential development. Today, the remaining 40 acres in the middle of the Genius Preserve have a conservation easement placed over them, and the historic Ward House and the packing house have been moved onto this land near the Wind Song estate home.

In 1999, the Charles Hosmer Morse Foundation released a request for proposals (RFP) for the purchase of the land. With the historical legacy of the property and its strategic location, one might expect a 25-plus page RFP. However, the foundation only issued one page seeking potential bidders, which included simple, direct instructions: Tell us who you are, what you have done before, what you think the property is worth, and how you plan to develop it.

After hearing news of the forthcoming RFP, I recognized the exceptional value and uniqueness of this property and decided I should try to purchase it. I was fortunate in that I knew the president of both foundations—Harold A. Ward. A lawyer at a prestigious downtown Winter Park law firm, Harold had deep ties to the Morse and McKean families for his entire life. It was his grandfather who built the historic wood-frame Ward House on the Genius Preserve, and his father, who had grown up there, became the property's caretaker. Harold Ward was the first in his family to attend college, and it was through the Rollins College board that I got to know him. Harold was the longest-serving Rollins Trustee member until he stepped down a few years ago, at which time I achieved that title. For 32 years, Harold and I served on the college board together.

Another factor also influenced my interest: About 20 years prior, with the recession ending around 1978, the Central Florida real estate market had regained strength. Buyers began purchasing land at retail prices and paid cash; therefore, it no longer made sense to speculate on undeveloped or raw land. In response, I adopted a new business model: If I bought land, I had to use it, whereas before, I would buy land and hold it as it appreciated in value over a number of years.

My first deal using this new business model involved a residential subdivision in Seminole County. The plan was to pay retail price for the land, subdivide it, and then sell the finished lots to home builders. I chose to focus on residential subdivisions because, if you buy 100 lots and only sell 50 because of one reason or another, then at least you would have sold half of the property. You would have liquidated part of the investment, and "self-liquidating" properties are easier to exit than a single-use income property. This was most prudent and, in my opinion, the most practical way to be in the real estate development business and maneuver through different market conditions.

By the time I became aware of the RFP from the Charles Hosmer Morse Foundation, I had been involved in approximately 10,000 single-family lots in Central Florida. However, this land in Winter Park was incredibly unique . . . and would be very expensive. This development would create 246 large residential lots in the middle of Winter Park, 40 of which would be situated on the three surrounding lakes, so indeed, it was very special.

As part of my plan to acquire and develop the foundation's property, I contacted a prominent real estate marketing group out of Richmond, Virginia, and Jacksonville, Florida, called East West Partners, which had vast experience in developing large, master-planned communities in the Southeast. Unlike East West Partners, I had never developed large residential communities, and even though the 160 acres would only contain 246 lots, I recognized it would be a very high-end project. For this reason, instead of selling the lots to production home builders, these lots would need to be sold to individual homeowners and custom home builders. This would involve a different type of real estate and development, and I needed assistance and expertise in this area.

Then, needing to secure a strong financial partner as well, I formed a partnership with a private equity group out of New York called DLJ Real Estate Capital Partners, which later became Credit Suisse First Boston. This partnership of Keewin, DLJ, and East West Partners then offered $35.5 million to the foundation, about five dollars per square foot of land—incredibly expensive, more or less the normal price for a commercial shopping center property, not a residential community.

Although our bid was not the highest offer, Harold Ward and the foundation's board chose to sell it to our partnership, knowing that I, being local and known in Winter Park, would be sensitive in developing this historic property and the communities surrounding the land. Once successful in the right to acquire the property, I suddenly thought of the saying about the dog that catches the car . . . *Now what do I do with it?*

CHAPTER 12
WINDSONG

"Windsong can only be likened to developing part of Central Park in New York City. From a residential perspective, nothing in my 46-year career of being involved in almost 20,000 single-family residential lots in Central Florida has been comparable."

One of the first parts of the development process was for Keewin, DLJ, and East West Partners to complete a pro forma for the project, using the proposal lot prices based on their location, size, and for some of the lots, lake frontage. Using $35.5 million for the land purchase and $15 million to develop the property, the pro forma showed that the $50 million project would be worth $72 million, resulting in a net profit of approximately $22 million. To put this into perspective, residential lots in Central Florida had an average value of $50,000 back then, whereby many of these lots in the heart of Winter Park would be worth approximately $400,000 each, an incredibly large number.

However, since this was truly a one-of-a-kind piece of property, we had no way of substantiating that value. Rather, we had to be intuitive or rely on our gut when projecting the final value and profit. We could look at what buyers were paying to purchase and tear down homes in the area, for no similar properties were like this in Florida, let alone Winter Park. I likened this property to developing part of Central Park in New York—how does one put a price on that?

Before the one-million-dollar escrow deposit became non-refundable, DLJ decided to hire a real estate research firm based in Atlanta, Georgia, to perform a market study in an attempt to confirm the lot values. This firm sent a young associate, who was about 22 years old with little experience, to conduct the market study. However, because the land was so unique, there was no way to accurately establish the value of the property. All that could be done was to talk with local Winter Park realtors and ask, "If you had these vacant lots to sell, what do you think clients would pay for them?" After collecting this data and because of the uniqueness of this property, they issued their market study report with a market value estimate at $45 million for all of the lots. A significant difference from our pro forma value of $72 million.

As an example, lakefront lots that we valued at $450,000 were valued at $210,000. These numbers were so far apart that all of our partners agreed to ignore the market study and continue with the acquisition. In addition, I negotiated with Ohio Savings Bank for a $35-million acquisition and development (A&D) loan with no personal liability, which was highly unusual in the development business. The bank provided the $35 million, DLJ invested $15 million, and our group contributed 5 percent of the DLJ total, or $750,000. The partnership now had the funds to purchase and develop the property.

In early 2000, we closed on the land and commenced site work construction. The name of the new community was to be called Windsong, derived from the estate home where Jeannette and Hugh McKean once lived.

The Entrance to Windsong

As part of the marketing plan for the lots, we formed an on-site captive real estate brokerage company called Windsong Realty, which would exclusively handle the sales of the Windsong houses as well as the lots where they were built. Also, as part of the "builder program," we assembled a group of six of Central Florida's best custom home builders who would be the exclusive home builders for all house construction within the community. Doing this ensured that each home was built with quality and care, a reflection of the special nature of the land. It also enabled us to create the overall aesthetic feel of Windsong. One thing we decided was that we did not want to create a neighborhood where all the houses looked identical. Each home needed to have a personality, distinguishable from its neighbors.

Our planned marketing strategy was unconventional, for usually, captive real estate companies require all of their homes to have the same features, such as barrel tile roofs. In Windsong, we took an opposite approach, instead mandating that houses side by side could not have barrel tile roofs. In fact, at least two houses had to separate the first barrel tile roof from the next, and the same went for other design features. One house could be modern, the next Spanish, and the one after that may be more of a cottage style. It was of the utmost importance that Windsong be different, eclectic, and inviting, patterned after the style of the rest of Winter Park. For the same reason, no front entrance walls were constructed, and all of the houses that sat on the perimeter of the property faced out toward the street and the established neighborhoods, rather than inward toward the other Windsong homes. Windsong thus became a *part* of this community, rather than exclusionary to the community.

Irrespective of our financial projections, the final gross revenue did not end up being $72 million (*or* $45 million). Instead, the Windsong residential community resulted in a $96 million gross sellout, an overwhelming success. Today, the total tax value of this one residential community has grown to $409 million ... from one small project.

As mentioned earlier, the opportunity to develop Windsong can only be likened to developing part of Central Park in New York City. From a residential perspective, nothing in my 46-year career of being involved in almost 20,000 single-family residential lots in Central Florida has been comparable. It is the heart of Winter Park and easily one of the most beautiful residential areas in Florida and beyond. Being the person who was selected to purchase and develop Windsong was a most unique opportunity—one that resulted in millions of dollars of housing, value, and a monumental centerpiece of this community.

CHAPTER 13
EXTERNAL FORCES

> "The investment in connections is much more dependable and resilient than any financial investment—and, as such, always pays dividends."

I first met Richard Swann, who later, at my recommendation, represented Universal Studios Florida, when he adopted the bank lawyer position at the bank where Larry Godwin went to work after leaving Barnett. From that point on, we had a long business and personal relationship with Richard, a relationship that included my first two residential real estate development deals in 1978. They were through and with Richard.

Because of this relationship, Larry and I were very involved in the business enterprise that Richard was building. This included the formation of a bank that became American Pioneer Savings Bank, which merged with Heritage Federal Savings and Loan Association in Daytona Beach. Along with the two banks, Richard acquired several other businesses, including an insurance company, a title insurance business, and a home-building business. These three companies were at the heart of his business enterprise, and as they all related to and fed off of each other, they became quite large over the years. The bank opened more branches and soon evolved into a regional player in the financial services sector, and the home-building company grew right alongside the title insurance company. As a testament to how much I believed in the work Richard was doing, I joined the board of the title insurance company and invested in American Pioneer's publicly traded stock.

By 1986, American Pioneer was issuing preferred shares. Anticipating the bank's expansion and therefore need for additional capital, a great number of people, myself included, took advantage of this opportunity and bought the bank's preferred stock. To make my investment easier, they arranged a loan for basically 100 percent financing from another bank, and since American Pioneer paid a dividend of 7 percent and the loan had a 6 percent interest rate, the bank's dividend would cover the interest.

This was considered a good investment with minimal risk. Of course, I had to personally guarantee the loan, but this was a simple way to acquire stock in this bank with good leverage.

Around this time, during the 80s, the Federal Reserve allowed interest rates to run high in an effort to stop rising inflation, which slowed the economy.[1] All banks got "lockjaw" and wanted to be paid back immediately. However, as the economy slowed, creating sources of revenue in order to repay loans was tougher. This environment is why banks are sometimes called "fair-weather friends." When things are good, they lend you money; when things are bad, they want the money back . . . and sometimes, the timing isn't optimal.

This all came to a head in 1989 when the government passed the Financial Institutions Reform, Recovery, and Enforcement

Act (FIRREA), which placed heavy restrictions on the savings and loan (S&L) industry. S&Ls were different from commercial banks; they were governed by the Federal Home Loan Bank Board and owned by borrowers and depositors or a group of shareholders, unlike commercial banks. Although S&Ls in the 1980s were smaller than banks, they acted as important entities for the US mortgage market. In 1980, almost 4,000 S&Ls had $600 billion in total assets, with about $480 billion in mortgage loans. This represented half of the $960 billion in outstanding home mortgages at that time.[2]

The FIRREA legislation included several new initiatives, but for purposes of this story, it is most pertinent to examine FIRREA's effect on "goodwill" with S&Ls.

Prior to 1989, goodwill enabled healthy S&Ls to merge with other S&Ls and commercial banks. In a typical merger, an S&L would merge with an existing S&L. If the regulatory capital of that S&L was, say, $20 million but the S&L making the acquisition had to pay $50 million for the merger, then the remaining $30 million would be classified as "goodwill" and could be written off over the next 40 years. Because this recapture spanned such a long period, it was easy to absorb this special "cost" or expense into the S&L's operations.

The introduction of FIRREA, however, put a limit on the amount of goodwill that could be counted as capital. The new act required S&Ls to write off all of the goodwill not in 40 years, but in 120 *days*. Institutions had benefited from the prior goodwill process for years with the encouragement of regulators. However, since the new FIRREA rules were not retroactive, institutions were not "grandfathered in."[3]

These new limitations led to what is called the S&L crisis of the late 1980s and 1990s. Across the country, $407 billion was lost as 747 S&Ls went out of business. In the wake of this crisis, the government established the Resolution Trust Corporation (RTC) in place of the abolished Federal Home Loan Bank Board and the thrifts' insurance fund. The RTC received the assets from the failed S&Ls and sold them at a large discount to private investors to help cover their losses.[4]

America Pioneer, the institution in which I had invested, was one of these impacted S&Ls. It had goodwill due to the acquisition of the bank in Daytona, among other business deals, and by the new rules, needed to pay it back immediately. The unfortunate fact is that before FIRREA was passed, American Pioneer was making money and doing good business. After FIRREA, it failed by 1990.[5]

At the same time, all the S&Ls and commercial banks attempted to collect loans in a weak economic environment. I had several loans with different banks, each of which had assets behind them. My American Pioneer loan, however, was secured by the S&L stock. Consequently, when the S&L crisis caused the failure of that stock, the worth of my collateral went to zero. I was shocked.

About 12 years into my career, I found myself at my lowest financial point—the first true test of my "relationships and reputation." Fortunately, I discovered that I had made the right choice in cultivating strong relationships. The investment in connections is much more dependable and resilient than any financial investment—and, as such, always pays dividends.

During this time, I had been on the board of BankFIRST, a regulated community bank board in Winter Park, for a number of years. The founder and majority owner of the bank, Jim Barnes, and I had known each other for quite some time. Not only did Keewin occupy office space in his building for 20 years, but I also held the position of chairman of the Winter Park board and vice chairman of BankFIRST's holding company board. Normally, if a board member at a regulated commercial bank became financially weakened, that person would have to step down from their role or be asked to exit the bank board. As such, I approached Jim Barnes, explained what happened, and told him that I needed to resign.

"I won't let you resign," he responded. "You're too valuable to the bank." It was as simple as that. I, along with two other board members, remained a part of what we called the bank's "kitchen cabinet," a trusted advisory group that consulted with Jim Barnes on key decisions. Together, we all grew BankFIRST into the second-most successful community bank in Central Florida and strategically planned to sell the bank in May 2007, whereby we received over four times the book value and achieved the second-highest sale price of a bank in the country. The transaction was simply amazing, especially being only a few months prior to the next major recession, so much so that I call it one of two "Grand Slam" investments I have made. Jim has continued to be one of my closest friends, and he has invested in virtually every investment deal I have made—another example of a deep and long-standing friendship.

Another significant relationship in my life was, and is, with Rollins College. However, if a large community institution such as Rollins had a deeply involved member become financially weakened, then in most cases, they would be asked to resign.

I approached the then president of Rollins, Rita Bornstein, and offered my resignation from the board of trustees, to which she said, "No way. I'm not letting you resign. You have to remain on the board." Obviously, it didn't hurt that I had chaired the search committee that had brought Rita to Rollins, but the bottom line was that she saw the big picture. My personal issue at the time was not important enough to have me leave the board of trustees.

I was most grateful and appreciative. Two very large and important entities in the Central Florida community chose to keep me involved despite my temporary financial difficulties. Because of this support, I did not miss a beat. Shortly thereafter, I did the second Universal Studios real estate deal, which was a series of major transactions that generated millions of dollars of commission income for me. I continued to do numerous investments after that as there was no impact to my reputation. Equally as important, there was no negative impact on any of my relationships. It turned out that my relationships were stronger than a financial setback, which allowed me time to completely recover in every area of my financial and professional life. I can look back now with perspective and see how this challenging period taught me important lessons. The years that followed from 1989 to 2008 brought unparalleled economic growth, and because of three key principles I learned, I was able to fully participate in it and more than recover.

In 2008, when the next recession arrived, I was prepared. First, I had learned my lesson about leverage and had become much more conservative. There was a real estate saying, "Oh, Lord, give me one more chance, and I promise I won't throw it away this time," and this became my motto. Seeing a hyper-recession on the horizon, we ceased doing business in the beginning of that period and instead used the time from 2008 to 2011 to make strategic acquisitions. Then, when the market recovered in 2011, I was better off than I was when going into that recession.

The second lesson I learned concerned not being Pollyanna-ish, or excessively optimistic about economic cycles, specifically with the thinking that they will never end. The fact is, they always end. While I certainly still take risks when acquiring property, I do so strategically. Regarding leverage, I brought in outside partners, and we went short instead of long, meaning we were in and out of our deal in a few years instead of going down a long path with minimal control and much more risk.

Lastly, I learned that it does not matter how smart you are, how good your deal is, or what kind of business you are in. Sometimes, there are external forces you cannot control. But if you have a principled reputation, and if you do everything in your power to uphold your values, relationships, and faith in your friends and business associates, you have a much stronger chance of coming out on the other side successfully.

CHAPTER 14
THE EXPRESSWAY AUTHORITY

"To do what we did . . . required a great amount of time and intentional decision-making. But that was the commitment we made, and we upheld it for the good of one of Florida's greatest attractions: its ecosystem."

During my career, I have been appointed to three major public boards by three different governors of Florida. First, Governor Reubin Askew appointed me to the Seminole Memorial Hospital board located in Sanford, Florida, in the mid-70s. Then, I was appointed by Governor Bob Graham (and later reappointed by Governor Bob Martinez) to the Valencia Community College Board, where I served for eight years and was chairman for four. After joining the Rollins College Board of Trustees in 1988, I felt a bit uncomfortable serving on two major educational boards at the same time, so I stepped down from my board position at Valencia in order to serve my alma mater. In 2001, Governor Jeb Bush nominated me to serve on the governing board of the Orlando-Orange County Expressway Authority (O-OCEA), and the governor asked me to chair the board in my first year. Normally, one would serve two years or longer before taking a chairman position, but with his ask, I accepted the role during my first year and acted as chairman for my entire seven-year tenure.

The most critical item on the O-OCEA agenda concerned a significant threat to the Orlando metropolitan area's ability to function as an easily navigable and well-planned urban city: the lack of a completed outer beltway.

Looking at a map, Orlando can be divided into four quadrants: northwest, northeast, southeast, and southwest. I-4 helps divide these quadrants by running through the middle of Orlando, extending from Tampa to the southwest to Daytona Beach to the northeast. Therefore, when heading "east" on I-4 through Orlando, you actually drive north. The second piece of the quadrant is the oldest and most central road to Orlando, State Road 408 (SR 408), officially named the Spessard L. Holland East-West Expressway and owned by the Central Florida Expressway Authority (the successor of O-OCEA). About 45 years ago, the Expressway Authority chose to condemn approximately 1,200 homes in order to build this road, a project that most likely would never come to fruition today. However, had they not done this, there would be no major east-west road through Orlando, which would have effectively paralyzed the community.

Despite these two major roads, Orlando was missing an integral piece. Almost every major metropolitan city has a beltway, a limited-access highway that encircles an urban area. Large cities like Houston, Texas, have several while others such as Jacksonville, Florida, have one but are now in the process of adding a second "outer" beltway.

For decades, Orlando had been planning to construct such a beltway around Central Florida. In fact, SR 417, the eastern road that runs from north to south, was originally intended to be a full beltway around Orlando. However, this road system was divided into SR 417 (the east side) and SR 429 (the west side) instead, for the beltway had a considerable gap in the northwestern quadrant. A large area of environmentally protected land and the Wekiva River created a major obstacle to completing this path and connecting this major regional highway to I-4, northwest of Orlando.

Rather than construct through this protected land to complete the beltway and connect to I-4, the plan when I joined the Expressway Board in 2000 was to direct this road to the northwest, up to the city of Mount Dora with no connection to I-4. This proposed road was to be called the Northwest Connector and would carry traffic in one direction and then stop at Mount Dora. While this spur road would relieve *some* traffic congestion from the northwest area, it did nothing to complete the much-needed beltway to I-4, which would be a much more effective solution to manage traffic and ensure Orlando is an easily accessible metropolitan area.

When I joined the Expressway Authority board, I saw this "spur route" as a very poor and nonoptimal solution. In my eyes, for Orlando to achieve the status of an important and major US city, the completion of the beltway was of the utmost importance. Fortunately, prior to joining the board, I had been actively involved in local, state, and national politics and deeply involved in the real estate development business for years, and I had encountered and navigated through sensitive environmental issues on numerous occasions. This is partially why I was immediately elected chairman of the board. It is also why I soon received a phone call from Charles Lee, the head of the Florida Audubon Society, an Orlando-based state-wide environmental conservation organization that advocates for the protection of land, water, wetlands, and wildlife.

"I want to bring a group from the environmental community together and see if, with your help and support, we can find a practical and feasible solution to complete the beltway," Mr. Lee said. I agreed, stating that I would also like for one of my fellow board members, the District Five secretary of the Florida Department of Transportation (FDOT), Mike Synder, to attend as well. The completion of this "missing link" and creation of a full expressway system was of supreme importance, so having this door opened by the environmental community, we were most excited with this opportunity.

The meeting was held soon after that phone call. In attendance were me, representing the Expressway Authority; Mike Synder, representing the FDOT; and 12 environmentalists, representing various conservation groups such as Friends of the Wekiva, the Florida Audubon Society, the Sierra Club, and the Nature Conservancy. Once we began the discussions, it became apparent that everyone in the room valued collaboration. My position was that a completed beltway, rather than the Northwest Connector, was imperative to Orlando and that it was worth all effort to work out an agreement with the environmental community. One might expect environmentalists to oppose that view, protesting any construction within these protected areas to reduce or eliminate the impact as much as possible. However, there were enough forward thinkers present to see the overall value of a completed beltway. Rather than debate the construction of the beltway through the wetlands and across the Wekiva River, they all agreed and stated their willingness to help find a compromise and solution. The process would be complicated and expensive, but this meeting established the path for Orlando to find a way to complete the beltway while prioritizing the protection of at-risk ecosystems.

We negotiated an agreement that allowed us to immediately suspend the planning work on the Northwest Connector and instead proceed with planning and designing a roadway that would lead to building the Western Beltway with the help of the environmental community. As part of this process and plan, Governor Bush formed a task force, which later became a commission, called the Wekiva River Basin Commission. I sat on this board with a number of environmental groups, engineers, planners, contractors, and other interested parties to establish the rules and protocols needed to build the "missing link" to this important regional road.

The Wekiva River and its basin are home to exceptionally diverse and abundant wildlife. A result of the limestone underlying Central Florida, the Wekiva River Aquatic Preserve has more than 30 springs, which form creeks and rivers that extend for miles through forested floodplains and swamps. This forms a complex ecological system of rivers, springs, lakes, streams, wetland prairies, and hardwood forests, where notable plants such as the red buckeye, chinquapin, and Carolina basswood are found. Protected bird species such as the wood stork, bald eagle, and sandhill crane build nests in trees along the river, and even hundreds of West Indian manatees populate certain areas within the springs.[1] Although each of these species and more were of high importance when considering construction, the primary concern for the Wekiva River Basin Commission, at the time, was the Florida black bear.

One of the largest populations of the Florida black bear, a threatened species, uses the land surrounding the Wekiva River to travel between the Ocala National Forest and the conservation lands that comprise the Wekiva-Ocala Greenway in Orange, Seminole, and Lake counties.[2] Prior to the construction of the beltway, these black bears were wandering onto the existing state highway (SR 46), which bisected their natural migration path, and many were either getting injured or killed by cars. Therefore, one of the key actions we had to take as a group was creating "bear overpasses" in the construction plan so that the black bears could cross under the road rather than take the risk of traveling across it. Every choice we made—what fencing we used, how we planned to build the bridge, etc.—took environmental protection into consideration, not simply for the bears but for Wekiva and its habitats as a whole.

This process was not only costly but complex. To do what we did, rather than simply build a road with none of these protections, required a great amount of time and intentional decision-making. But that was the commitment we made, and we upheld it for the good of one of Florida's greatest attractions: its ecosystem. The Expressway Authority board began this initiative in 2001, which I led until stepping down from my board position in 2007. In 2024, the beltway was finally finished and connected to I-4, and Orlando now has a fully functional regional beltway around the entire metropolitan area.

Although I played a key role in initiating the process, the Expressway Authority needed to be in full agreement. I was fortunate to have two amazing fellow board members who supported me throughout, particularly fellow board member Orlando Evora, who is one of my closest friends today. For my seven years on the Expressway board as chairman, he was my vice chairman. Subsequently, he joined the Catholic Foundation board with me and the Rollins College board, where he is a key leader. The other gentleman was Arthur Lee, a good entrepreneur in the hospitality business who was nothing but a key supporter throughout this process.

Without that first meeting 23 years ago and without those formative and impactful collaborative efforts, Central Florida would almost certainly be without a completed beltway around Orlando today. It is community projects like this that make me proud to live here and, more than that, proud to help my community grow responsibly.

CHAPTER 15
THE ALFOND INN

"I donate my time to these organizations not to receive anything in return, but because I want to give back to my community and make a difference."

At one time during my career, when I was out of my mind I suppose, I simultaneously managed three substantial community roles: chairman of the Orlando-Orange County Expressway Authority, a $200-million-dollar regional transportation organization; chairman of the Winter Park Health Foundation, a $120-million-dollar charitable foundation; and chairman of the Board of Trustees of Rollins College. While some may hesitate to take on the responsibilities of one such job, I took on all three. Looking back with some perspective, I recognize it was an unusual decision, but I found all three roles to be fulfilling and exciting while making a meaningful impact on the Central Florida community.

Whenever I told someone about my concurrent board responsibilities, they would first ask, "Are you crazy?" Then, they would usually follow that question with, "How do you get any work done?"

To which I responded, "I luckily have loyal and active business partners." Because my partners handled the brunt of the work at Keewin, I was able to dedicate more time to these interests. One of those interests has always been education, ever since my time as a student at Rollins.

With 36 years of experience on the Rollins College Board of Trustees, I am not the oldest, but I am currently the longest-serving board member. I am also the only person to have served two non-consecutive terms as board chairman throughout the 136 years of the college's history.

Upon joining the board in 1988, I was immediately asked to chair the search committee for the 13th president of Rollins. After a long and detailed process, we chose Rita Bornstein. Years later, I was asked again to chair the search committee for the 15th president, and we chose Grant Cornwell. As chairman of the search committee, you develop a close relationship with the selected candidate because you are the one overseeing their recruitment, hiring, and introduction to the college. I have always felt especially close to these two presidents whom I helped recruit. In fact, after President Bornstein's unfortunate passing in January 2024, I had the honor and privilege of being one of the four people who got to speak about her life at her memorial service.

Rita was Rollins's first female president and was known for her eminent fundraising abilities, securing $160.2 million in gifts that supported the college's efforts over the course of her tenure.[1] She was a respected mentor, adviser, and colleague, not to mention a brilliant leader. President Cornwell, set to retire in June 2025, has likewise achieved great strategic initiatives for the college, including a program to prepare students for their careers, a reimagination of the Crummer Graduate School of Business's curriculum, and the construction of a 500-bed lakefront residential complex, to name a few. To this day, I consider Rita Bornstein and Grant Cornwell the greatest presidents Rollins has ever had.

My work as part of the Rollins trustees board has resulted in many special opportunities, but one in particular stands as one of my proudest achievements: the chance to chair the ad hoc committee that originally developed The Alfond Inn in Winter Park in 2013.

About 15 years ago, the board of trustees held a strategic planning meeting. We used a scatter board concept, a planning tool on a large board with two axes. The top left axis on the board listed the easiest goals to accomplish while the top right showed the most difficult. Then, the bottom axis showed the most impactful objectives and the least impactful in the bottom left. When deciding which initiatives to pursue, the board of trustees wanted to refrain from projects that were the "easiest" but "least impactful." So, looking at the seven or so projects we identified, one project stood out as the most difficult but the most rewarding: building an inn and conference facility for Rollins College.

Most prominent universities and colleges, big or small, have an inn or hotel associated with that college. Rollins wanted such a facility so that parents of students could find a close place to stay for Alumni Weekend, Parent Weekend, graduations, and other events. In addition, prospective students and their families from out of state needed a local hotel when they came to tour the school, for very few options existed in Winter Park at that time. Thus, our principal goal became finding land to build a hotel from the ground up.

During a break from that same meeting, I called a friend of mine whose boss owned a strategic piece of land. About a block from the Rollins campus, the 60-year-old Langford Hotel had been sold and torn down a few years before. The new owners had been attempting to build a hotel on the land for several years yet never accomplished this goal. Instead, a luxury condominium project was constructed on a part of the site, with the vacant land of three and a half acres next to it.

I asked what the plans were for this land and explained that the college may have an interest in it. He responded that they would love to sell the property to Rollins, and further said that the timing could not have been more perfect. Hanging up the phone, I told him we would be in touch. Three months later, we purchased the land for $9.9 million.

The college bought the land without any plans for the hotel or any idea of how many rooms would be needed. We had no expertise in the hotel business, nor did we have a hospitality school on campus. Rather, we bought it purely in good faith and knew that without this parcel of land, we could not even begin to consider creating an inn or conference facility.

At that point, the board formed an ad hoc committee, and I was named chairman. The next point of business was hiring consultants and a fee developer to provide specialized expertise. We also put out a request for qualifications (RFQ), looking for a partner in the lodging industry. And although six major hotel developers and owners responded, we found that every respondent's plan included borrowing against our debt-free property to pay for the construction of the hotel—thereby introducing an unnecessary liability to Rollins. If something went wrong, the college would have had to pay off the debt or risk losing the property, which would also mean the loss of the initial $9.9 million investment. It was at this point that we considered developing the inn ourselves.

Rollins College had previously developed a major retail-commercial building called the SunTrust Plaza, now called Truist Plaza, on Park Avenue about 15 years prior. I had also served on that committee and remembered the process we followed: We hired a consultant and built and developed the project ourselves. We had to hire an architect, a management company, and others ... and then we had to find a way to fund it.

In 1956, a gentleman named Harold Alfond purchased an old woolen mill in Dexter, Maine, and founded Dexter Shoe Company, following in his father's footsteps in the shoe manufacturing business. He is credited with the invention of the factory outlet store as he was the first to open a store to sell his own "factory seconds," i.e., factory-made shoes that did not pass the quality inspection, in the 1960s. By the 1990s, the Dexter Factory Outlet chain had expanded to over 80 stores, employed over 4,000 people, manufactured over 36,000 pairs of shoes daily, and generated more than $250 million in annual sales. As a result, the chain was approached by many companies looking to acquire it.

Alfond declined many offers to purchase Dexter, not wanting the new ownership to depart from his family-oriented way of running the business by expanding into foreign manufacturing. Therefore, when Berkshire Hathaway, a multinational conglomerate run by Warren Buffett, presented Alfond with an agreement that promised to maintain his current management style, Alfond finally agreed to sell the business.

In 1993, Dexter and its affiliates were sold for $433 million in Berkshire Hathaway stock.

Harold Alfond believed, "Whatever you can give, you've got to give. You've got to make your town better, you've got to make your state better, you've got to make everyone better because they can't get by on promises." This is demonstrated by his establishment of the first private foundation in Maine in 1950, the Harold Alfond Foundation.[2]

Though based in Maine, it is this foundation that helped fund the Rollins inn, now named The Alfond Inn, by contributing a $12.5 million grant.[3] The initial $9.9 million investment for the land and construction costs resulted in a total project cost of $45 million, with Rollins putting up approximately $25 million to cover the remaining expenses. After agreeing on and accomplishing several decision points, The Alfond Inn opened its doors in August 2013.[4] Our initial pro forma contained 115 rooms, operating at an occupancy rate of 64 percent at an average room price of $165 per night. And from the beginning, it was a monumental success.

Combining its branding as a "boutique hotel" with the uniqueness brought by the Alfond family's art purchases, there was no other inn like it in Central Florida. Harold and Bibby Alfond's eldest son, Ted, graduated from Rollins College in 1968, as did his wife, Barbara. As noted art collectors and patrons of several art institutions, the two donated the Alfond Collection of Contemporary Art, a collection that has increased to a value of $12 million, to the inn. Rather than purchase and display standard hotel "screw-on" art pieces, The Alfond Inn features museum-quality artworks. As in a museum, this art collection is so large that the inn cannot display every piece at once. Instead, it must rotate artworks. Very quickly, The Alfond Inn established a reputation as "an art museum with rooms attached." Staying at the inn became very sought-after, and soon after opening, it continually ran at an occupancy rate above 90 percent both on weekends and during the week due to conferences, weddings, and business meetings.

The Alfond Inn has become an absolute financial success, a significant financial benefit for Rollins College, and an opportunity for the college's students. While working with the Harold Alfond Foundation in the planning and development of the inn, Rollins agreed that 100 percent of the net operating income would fund scholarships to create the Alfond Scholars Program over the course of 25 years. Then, once the 25-year term ends, the net operating income would begin funding Rollins College's general operating budget. Since the inn's opening 10 years ago, the Alfond Scholars Program now annually awards up to 10 full scholarships that include tuition and an unlimited meal plan to first-year students. With Rollins giving away 5 percent per year of the endowment balance through the Alfond Scholars Program, the inn currently provides approximately $280,000 for students over four years, a sum that will continue to grow.[5]

In late 2023, The Alfond Inn added 71 rooms to the initial 112, in addition to a new 3,000-square-foot spa, cafe and wine bar, and swimming pool. It has been ranked as one of the best hotels in Florida by *Travel + Leisure*, *U.S. News & World Report*, and *Condé Nast Traveler*. Additionally, it has the coveted AAA Four Diamond Rating from the AAA.[6] The Alfond Inn has become a highly successful Winter Park asset and is undoubtedly one of Rollins College's, and one of my own, most prized accomplishments.

Looking back on this time when I headed three separate community organizations in addition to Keewin, I first wonder how I had the energy. Then, I consider how fortunate I am to have such dedicated business partners. I view this time in my life as one of the most interesting and productive, for I never intentionally set out to accept such a challenge. These separate opportunities simply presented themselves to me, and I was lucky enough to be able to see them through. The question of "why" is often asked to me though, and in response, I tell the same story.

Once, while serving on the Expressway Authority board, I was invited to Milan, Italy, to discuss the value of toll roads as part of a panel. In Europe, most toll roads are privately owned by profit-making companies that build roads and collect tolls, the net proceeds of which are then returned to their investors. This is in contrast to America, where almost all toll roads are owned by the government or quasi-public entities, and the profits go back into building and maintaining more roads. As most Europeans see America as the most private-enterprise-centric country in the world, the public nature of our toll roads surprised the European panelists, who expected the structure to be the exact opposite. Therefore, I was asked to go to Milan to explain the benefits of "public" toll roads, sharing how the Expressway Authority was able to borrow tax-exempt funds as a government entity and how that reduced our borrowing cost.

It was then that someone in the audience asked a question: "How much do you get paid?"

To which I responded, "Nothing."

"Yeah, yeah, okay. But how do you get reimbursed?" they asked.

"I don't get anything. It's public service," I reiterated.

The concept was foreign to this audience. The question-asker even went on to imply that I must somehow receive "under-the-table" compensation, but I reaffirmed the truth: I donate my time to these organizations not to receive anything in return, but because I want to give back to my community and make a difference. It was also an additional benefit that from healthcare to transportation to education, each board that I chaired was different, engaging, and served an important community role. I am a hardcore businessman, but quite frankly, it was fun to be a part of important decisions and to help people in a variety of ways—ways that I was able to experience because I said yes to these organizations that asked for my help, no matter how "out of my mind" I seemed to the outside world.

CHAPTER 16
MISTER ROGERS

"The kind of students we want to have at Rollins are thoughtful and contributory people who want to go out, make money, and help the world. Exactly as Mister Rogers did."

During the time after I was chairman of the Rollins College Board of Trustees but an active member of the board, an opportunity presented itself to establish a lasting monument on campus, one that would become a top attraction in Central Florida and be visited by people from all over the country and world.

The events leading up to this opportunity all seem very serendipitous when I look back. It all started when my wife, Linda, and I were on a barge canal trip in Burgundy, France, with friends. We were six passengers along with six crew members on this barge, which made for an intimate and unique experience. During the trip, we traveled through canals built in the 1800s and often stopped for excursions using the van that followed our barge down the waterway. The barge moved at such a glacial, peaceful pace that the ducks swimming beside the boat were faster than us.

Each day, the captain and his wife (our hostess) would give us a preview of possible excursions while we sat in the full-sized living room located on the barge. Whether we wished to stop in the town of Dijon, visit a vineyard, or experience another attraction, we only had to ask. On one such occasion, sitting with the other couples, the captain and his wife brought to our attention a coffee table book that featured numerous bronze sculptures. Drawing our attention to one sculpture in particular, they told us they knew the artist well and that he lived nearby, close to Dijon. They asked us if we cared to visit his studio and gallery. Since we didn't have anything pressing to do, we agreed, having never heard of the artist, a man named Paul Day.

Although I have a reasonably good knowledge of paintings, particularly impressionism, I did not know anything about sculptures. We were just excited to go along for the ride. When we arrived at the artist's studio, we discovered that Paul was abroad in the Czech Republic, working with one of his foundries. However, his wife, Catherine, was there, so she took us to tour his studio and gallery. By the time we left, we had become very impressed by Paul's work.

The next day, the captain told us that Paul was back home and wanted to stop by for a glass of wine. Once again motivated by the *laissez-faire*, we said, "Why not?" Paul came to our barge and conversed with us for a few hours. We found out he was a Brit living in France and that he was fairly famous, having made the Iraq and Afghanistan Memorial, the Queen Mother Memorial, and the Battle of Britain Monument, all located in London. Perhaps most excitingly, Paul was the sculptor behind the famous statue, *The Meeting Place*, in the even more famous train station, the St. Pancras Station in London.

Guided by fate once again, it just so happened that St. Pancras Station was our next destination after the canal barge. Ever since I can remember, I have wanted to take the Eurostar across the English Channel from Paris to London, perhaps known to Americans by its more colloquial name, the Chunnel. Therefore, when we decided to go to London for three days after France, I highly anticipated this high-speed train journey. What I did not know was that the Chunnel would transport us directly to the St. Pancras Station, the same station that proudly displays Paul Day's most celebrated sculpture.

We stepped off the train, and there it was: *The Meeting Place*, a 30-foot masterpiece depicting an endearing scene of a man and woman embracing. If its height had not already caught my attention, there was an immense neon sign positioned above the statue that did. The neon sign read, "I want my time with you," in a large, romantic script for everyone to read when they descended from the trains. The sign also caught my eye because I couldn't help but feel like I had seen that same artwork before. After a little more thought, I realized it looked similar to several neon signs in The Alfond Inn.

The two neon signs at The Alfond read, "Everything for love," and "I remember everything you taught me here." As I had a hand in creating The Alfond Inn and because I had spent many days there for lunches, dinners, and events, I was very familiar with the neon art, so I decided to research my hunch. To my amazement, after googling both locations, the neon sign at St. Pancras Station was created by the same artist who created the neon art at The Alfond Inn, Tracey Emin.

At this moment, another light bulb went on in my head. I realized that the Alfonds, those who curated the special art collection at The Alfond Inn, really knew what they were doing. Here I was halfway across the world, staring at a magnificent piece of art that had a connection to Rollins College. As my wheels continued to turn, I became intrigued with the idea of potentially commissioning a sculpture for Rollins College, and I knew just the man for the job: Paul Day.

Before I could commission Paul, I had to have an idea of what I wanted the sculpture to depict. This answer came to me more easily than any other piece of this puzzle. The sculpture had to be of Rollins College's most famous alumni: Mister Rogers.

Mister Rogers was by far Rollins's most widely known graduate. We already had a couple of ways to honor him on campus. There was a section at the library displaying his iconic sweater and sneakers, and every year, there was a Mister Rogers Walk. But by and large, Rollins did not have anything of real significance to pay tribute to this great man. In my mind, a sculpture could be the perfect memorial. I just needed to convince everyone else of this idea.

When I returned home from Europe, the first person I called was Barbara Alfond. Barbara, in conjunction with her family's Harold Alfond Foundation, had financed the building of The Alfond Inn, and she and her husband, Ted, had personally curated the significant amount of art within the hotel. Knowing her passion for and immense familiarity with art, I told her my idea, hoping to hear her opinion on the project and gain her interest in its execution. She thought it was a great idea, but she told me that I should discuss the idea with the president of Rollins, Grant Cornwell. This step did not deter me in any way, for I was very close to the president because I was the chairman of the search committee that brought him to Rollins.

I described what I was envisioning to President Cornwell, and he expressed his approval. However, what he did not say in so many words, but implied, was that the college did not have the current financial capacity to fund the sculpture. If I wanted to see this through, it would be up to me to raise the funds.

Before moving forward with the project, I needed to make sure we had a sculptor, so I reached out to Paul Day to see if he was interested and willing to do a sculpture of Mister Rogers.

His response: "Who's that?"

Living mostly in England and France, he had never heard of the American icon. I tried to explain Fred Rogers as best I could, and in the end, Paul agreed to undertake the commission.

For the piece itself, I had envisioned an image of Mister Rogers standing and holding his famous puppet, Daniel Tiger, and as such, I estimated the price would be around $250,000. Paul signed the contract I presented and then started on his own quest to research everything there was to know about Mister Rogers. He read articles, watched at least 100 episodes of *Mister Rogers' Neighborhood*, visited the Rollins campus, and talked to anyone who knew anything about him. Paul even went to Pittsburgh, talked to Mrs. Rogers, and met with people from the Fred Rogers Institute in Latrobe, Pennsylvania. He gathered all of this information in order to figure out what the sculpture should be. Eventually, he came back to me with a clay model of what he envisioned, a model that I have to this day. It was really unique: Mister Rogers with seven children.

Before Paul created this work of art, there were only two other prominent statues of Mister Rogers in existence. Located on the river in Pittsburgh, one portrays Mister Rogers sitting by himself, is over 10 feet tall, and was created by famous artist Robert Berks.

The other, in the James H. Rogers Memorial Park, is a sculpture depicting Rogers on a park bench, also sitting alone. Neither of these *really* depicted the real Fred Rogers, who was *always* around children. Anywhere he went, he was swarmed by kids, and he made it his mission to entertain and play with them.

Though more accurate to who Mister Rogers was as a person, the addition of seven new figures to the work created an issue. I knew that a statue of Mister Rogers standing alone with a puppet would be much cheaper than Mister Rogers with seven kids. I tried to convince Paul we only needed two kids, but he disagreed. I tried negotiating Paul down to four kids, and once again, he resisted. He convinced me that there needed to be seven kids, and in doing so, the price of the sculpture more than doubled, but the result was spectacular.

To raise money for this project, I first donated my own money and then reached out to friends, classmates, charitable foundations (including the Fred Rogers Foundation), and other friends of Rollins College. One of the donations came about from a happenstance conversation I had at the White House Christmas party the same year I was raising the money. Betsy DeVos, of the DeVos family, was at the event, and I knew she had a son who had attended Rollins. Serendipitously, I also knew that after my wife and I left the barge canal back in Burgundy, Dick and Betsy DeVos were the very next group to travel on the exact same barge. Incredible coincidence.

I started talking to Betsy about Winter Park, Rollins, and also our coinciding barge trips. I asked her if she had met Paul Day, and she explained they were big fans, her husband in particular being an admirer of his work. When I began to tell her about the Rollins sculpture, she said that she already knew about it, for Paul had told them. This coincidence led to members of the DeVos family donating $100,000 toward the project. All told, I raised a little over $800,000 for the eight-foot-tall, 3,000-pound, bronze sculpture not only to pay Paul but also to pay for the materials, display, landscaping, and lighting of the sculpture.

The president of the college and I only had one final task left: to find a unique spot on campus for the sculpture. We chose a spot in the courtyard between the Rollins Chapel and the Annie Russell Theater—the perfect location because, after Fred Rogers left Rollins, he became an ordained minister before moving on to a career on the screen and stage.

After the money was raised, it was all (figuratively and literally) in Paul's hands, and he could not have done a more phenomenal job. If you see the statue today, you will notice that the face of Mister Rogers looks so lifelike, almost as if it is a photograph. The veins on his hands and the wrinkles on his sweater make it seem as if he could stand up and begin walking at any moment.

Standing Next to the Mister Rogers Statue

The Mister Rogers Statue at Rollins

The sculpture is 360 degrees, with images on the back consisting of his beloved characters, like King Friday XIII, Queen Sara, X the Owl, and Trolley. Also, if you look at the expressions on the children's faces, you can see the real joy there. The sculpture is so dynamic, primarily due to Paul's talent and intentionality. If you look closely, there is a child just left of Rogers in a wheelchair. There is a famous story of a child in a wheelchair being in an early episode of *Mister Rogers' Neighborhood* and then meeting Rogers again about 30 years later. This is why Paul added the wheelchair—to honor the history of the show and partially to honor my oldest daughter, who also uses a wheelchair.

I am extremely proud of this monument that sits on the Rollins campus today. The legacy of Mister Rogers embodies everything Rollins stands for. He was kind, gentle, and considerate, and he looked at life in the most positive way. The kind of students we want to have at Rollins are thoughtful and contributory people who want to go out, make money, and help the world. Exactly as Mister Rogers did.

With this in mind, there was no other person whom I would have chosen to honor in this way. As I said, he was our most famous graduate with a long connection to Winter Park, but the reason why his name immediately came to mind when this idea formed in my head was because I had the privilege of meeting Fred and Joanne Rogers years ago at a Winter Park dinner. He was everything that I had expected he would be. The dinner was at the 13th President of Rollins Rita Bornstein's house, and Linda and I were there with Fred and Joanne Rogers and Rita and her husband. During the evening, he was very gracious, humble, and soft-spoken. Afterwards, he wrote a personal note to both of my children telling them how wonderful life was. We still have those notes today, framed in our home.

Although that was the only instance in which I met Fred, I was quite close to Joanne Rogers as she and I sat on the Rollins Board of Trustees together for about 15 years. We were so close that when the Tom Hanks film, *A Beautiful Day in the Neighborhood*, premiered in Pittsburgh in 2019, Joanne invited Linda and me there so that we could sit with her while we watched the movie.

Sadly, Joanne Rogers died in January of 2021, three months before the Mister Rogers sculpture was unveiled. Although she never saw the finished work of art, I am glad she was able to visit with Paul Day and provide him insights into Fred Rogers's life. If you look closely at the sculpture, you can see that on the bottoms of a couple of the children's shoes, there is an inscription that reads, "143." This was the code that Fred and Joanne would use to say, "I love you," because the numbers correspond with the letters in the phrase.

On the day of the dedication of the statue, there were 350 people in attendance. At the dinner afterward, we played a voicemail left by Yo-Yo Ma, a very dear friend of Fred and Joanne. He had left a voicemail discovered on Joanne's phone after she died, for at the time, Yo-Yo Ma did not realize the severity of her health and assumed she was only sick. The message was recovered by her son, John, who gave it to me. In it, Yo-Yo Ma tells Joanne that she's going to get through this and starts to play her a song. Without pausing, the song slowly turns into "Amazing Grace." It was a real tearjerker.

When we played the video at the dedication dinner, there was not a dry eye in the house. A beautiful moment and the perfect way to celebrate the lives of Fred and Joanne, which was always the true purpose behind this long journey of creating this sculpture. One that I would happily do again.

CHAPTER 17
THE KUMMER-KILBOURNE HOUSE

"Being part of a lasting landmark in Winter Park has been an honor for the last decade, and I take pride in the work we did to restore this property and honor its heritage."

Relationships and reputation can impact every part of doing business, sometimes even in determining your office space. When I started Keewin, I had an office on Park Avenue before eventually moving to an office with Jim Barnes in the BankFIRST building. I was perfectly happy in that office, staying there for 20 years.

One day, my assistant at the time, Sherry Cooper, received a call from a man who said he knew me from Rollins and my church, St. Margaret Mary Catholic Church. He mentioned that he and his daughter had a listing on a unique property downtown, and they wanted to know if I would be interested in buying it. Initially, I was skeptical because the deal did not seem relevant to my professional interests at the time, and it was unusual to hear about an available property from a phone call. However, because they knew me from Rollins and my church, I agreed to meet with them.

The day the father and daughter came into my office, I recognized them immediately. I knew the daughter, Tessa Hahn, from her time at Rollins and her father, Bob Hahn, because he was a well-known land planner in Central Florida and had been on the Winter Park Planning and Zoning Board. They handed me a single sheet of paper that was only printed on one side. On it were the words "Historic Home for Sale," a picture of a house, three or four facts, and the price: $960,000. Later, I would find out that they had printed this piece of paper the night before so that they would have a "brochure" to show me for this meeting. I still have that piece of paper today.

The building was constructed in 1916, such that it has been a part of Winter Park for more than 100 years. For the 50 years prior to my meeting with the Hahns, people had been trying to buy this property because it was in downtown Winter Park, 30 feet off of Park Avenue—a highly valuable location. Most interested parties wanted to buy it so that they could tear it down and build something bigger. I had known about the house for decades but had assumed it would stay in the family. You can imagine my surprise when I saw that very house on their "brochure."

I asked the Hahns about their relationship with the owners. Bob and Tessa had befriended the two remaining heirs to the home: two sisters who had lost their mother in 2012. Their mother had moved into the house when she was three years old and had died there at 97. The sisters asked Bob and Tessa to help them sell the property. Finding a buyer would have been a simple feat as they were not lacking in interested parties; in fact, people wanted to buy the house so badly that they would place multiple contracts into their mailbox. Despite this overwhelming interest, the remaining family wished for the new owner to preserve the home's history. Because of my relationships and reputation at Rollins and St. Margaret Mary Church, the Hahns approached me with the very special proposition.

When I realized they wanted me to buy the property, I said, "You're kidding. This can be bought?" I was so surprised that I asked twice: "This can be bought?"

They responded, "Yes, it can be."

Without any hesitation, I said, "I'll buy it."

I was the first and only person who the Hahns had talked to. With that verbal agreement and more or less no negotiations, I entered into a contract with the heirs, and a few months later, I purchased the property.

It was very important to the two heirs, and to me, that this historic building was protected and preserved. With this in mind, and because the building needed major renovations, I took my renovation plans to the historical board in Winter Park. Everyone on that committee was generally anti-development and may have been quick to assume that all I wanted to do was tear down the existing structure and build a new 10,000-square-foot building on the site. However, my plans demonstrated just the opposite. As an indication of this commitment, I had the property put on the National Register of Historic Properties, and I had the as-built drawings to show what the building looked like on the lot. Then, I proceeded to donate an easement over a 10-inch strip that was around the perimeter of the historic building to the city of Winter Park. This façade easement was instrumental in restricting changes to the exterior structure, and by doing this, I ensured that no one could ever make wholesale changes to the special property.

Since I intended to make this house Keewin's office, the interior needed renovations. First, the wood floors were black, so they needed to be stripped and resanded. The house also needed new plumbing, electrical, and air conditioning. I had an expert contractor for these needed changes, a friend named Hal George. I also had a close friend, John Cunningham, a most talented and experienced architect, prepare the necessary drawings for the renovation work. Fortunately, none of the work required any substantial alterations to the physical building. The only exception to this was taking down one wall and adding two walls to create my and my assistant Marcia's office. While doing so, the contractors found a hidden brick chimney that not even the lady who lived there her whole life knew about, which meant the chimney was from before 1916. This chimney is now a prominent and beautiful addition to the house.

Contractors also discovered that this building was made of two-by-fours of heart pine. Since the house was built in 1916, the lumber used to make this house would have been planted in Winter Park around the 1860s. Heart pine is very hard, almost petrified. Because we would never want to waste such unique wood, we replaced the iron staircase spindles with spindles made from the heart of pine wood. The iron spindles were added to the house in the 1940s without historical considerations. Milling this hard wood proved difficult as we broke 13 blades during the process. The outcome was worth the effort though, for replacing the spindles made the staircase totally authentic. At the end of the renovations, we only impacted just under 10 percent of the original structure.

Since 2013, the Kummer-Kilbourne House has been Keewin's office, and we enjoy it daily. An entire wall in the hallway is designated as our "historic hallway" and is full of pictures from the family's past, including interesting photos of when the family was in the business of constructing pine boxes and concrete burial vaults. Since Winter Park was expanding during the 30s, the family changed their business model to the lumber industry and created the Kummer Lumber Company, selling building materials that were used for their own home. By 1954, the house belonged to David and Christine Kummer-Kilbourne and their children, who lived there until 2012. Now, as Keewin's office, the Kummer-Kilbourne House is the last private home still standing on or near Park Avenue and downtown Winter Park.

In 2016, the house turned 100 years old, and we threw a large party with over 250 people in attendance. Being part of a lasting landmark in Winter Park has been an honor for the last decade, and I take pride in the work we did to restore this property and honor its heritage.

The Kummer-Kilbourne House (ca. 1916)

To this day, at least two or three times a week, someone will ask, "How in the world did you get this property?" A ton of people would have jumped at the opportunity to purchase this house if it had gone to an auction. Ironically, I didn't seek the house out; it seemed to fall in my lap.

I often tell people it was fate. And I recently said that to a friend, who replied, "Allan, do you know what the definition of fate is?"

I said, "Luck or good fortune?"

She looked back at me and said, "No. It's God's way of remaining anonymous."

CHAPTER 18
FAITH, FAMILY, AND FRIENDS

"Family relationships are the most worth having and by far the best deal you could ever make."

More than business, more than any chairmanship or memorial, the people I care for will always be the most important part of my life. The motto, "Faith, Family, and Friends," is displayed on a small sign sitting at the top of my office TV screen.

When it comes to friends, I have had the privilege of having a number of business partners who were also dear friends. Larry Godwin, who founded Keewin with me, was my close friend at the bank well before we became partners. After a number of years, he ended up leaving Keewin to go back to the home-building business, but we always remained close. After Larry's departure in 1992, Jay Folk became my business partner for the next 20 years. I originally met Jay as he was involved in the second real estate investment I completed back in 1975 when I purchased the 26 acres adjacent to Golden Grove, giving us another large parcel of valuable land on US 441 to sell. After that transaction, Jay and I became close friends and neighbors for a long time.

In fact, our kids grew up together. When Larry departed from Keewin, it was an easy choice to ask Jay to join me. He became the president of Keewin while I was the chairman and founder, and together, we completed some of the best deals of my career. Sadly, Larry, Jay, and my brother all passed away in 2012. Larry battled lymphoma for years, and Jay died unexpectedly from liver cancer. In the same year, I lost the three most important men in my life.

Upon Jay's death, Steve Rosser joined me as my business partner (and president of Keewin) for the last 12 years. I met Steve because he was our principal contact with one of our builder clients, Ryan Homes. He was involved in a new subdivision development that we completed with Ryan, and I immediately recognized his talent. Married with three kids, Steve was a civil engineer with a degree from Georgia Tech, had worked for three other major home builders, and had a great reputation in the market. About five years ago, Steve brought on our third partner, McKinzie Terrill, who happens to be the same age as the company. McKinzie and Keewin both celebrated their 45th birthdays in 2023. McKinzie, a lawyer by trade, had worked for several major home builders for 10 years. I first met him when he was negotiating with us on the *other* side of a deal. And that turned out to be a highly successful transaction. Now, with Steve and McKinzie, I have the two best real estate folks in the business as my partners.

At the center of the "Faith, Family, and Friends" motto, though, is family, and I wouldn't have my family if it weren't for meeting my wonderful wife, Linda, at a party in 1977. Linda and I were single when we met, although we both had dates the night of our mutual friend's party. I don't know how we started talking, but soon enough, we were deep into a three-hour conversation, both of us ignoring our dates as they became progressively irritated. Soon, I learned that Linda did not drink, eat much, or smoke, unlike me. She spent her life helping people as a nurse.

She wasn't just any nurse, either. She had an impressive job as the hospital's assistant administrator for a major hospital in Orlando, Orlando Regional (then called Orange Memorial Hospital). That wasn't where she thought her life would take her when she grew up in Iowa. Although she earned her undergraduate and master's degrees in nursing from the University of Iowa, she wanted to be a medical doctor, which later changed to pursuing a PhD in anatomy. To her complete surprise, a kerfuffle involving falsified research by her principal professor forced her to end her studies. She left the university, not wanting to be tainted with these fraudulent actions, and even though she had nearly completed her PhD, she moved to Orlando, which was, also, a warmer place to be.

Linda started working at Orange Memorial. She was an extremely qualified nurse, for while pursuing her PhD, she had taught doctors how to give physicals. Because of how knowledgeable and qualified she was, she became head nurse quickly and had 1,500 nurses working under her. People used to say that a head nurse is usually an "old battle-axe." I'd say Linda certainly wasn't an "old battle-axe"; she was a "young battle-axe!" But she had to be, for her job was not for the faint of heart. Shortly thereafter, she was promoted by the head of the hospital to become an assistant administrator, and she was put in charge of the nursing department, the emergency room, the psych unit, the neonatal unit, and their satellite hospital that was called the

"Hospital for Disney" located just off of Sand Lake Road, the nearest hospital to Disney World.

Suffice it to say, Linda had a most demanding job with many responsibilities and pressures. If there was ever any issue with a surgeon in an operating room, Linda was summoned on her beeper at any hour of the day or night. The easy fixes were taken care of at the hospital, and Linda would only be contacted when there was a problem or issue that only she could solve.

With a strong will and an interesting life based on her life's passion, it is no wonder that we talked for so long the first night we met. When it was time to part company, at my request, she wrote down her phone number and her name, Linda Wilson, on my pack of matches, and we went our separate ways. Then, I went home to my condo, threw the matches on the credenza, and that was that. I don't really know why, but I never called her.

Six months later, as part of my duties as chairman of the board of Seminole Memorial Hospital, I went to Atlanta, Georgia, to attend the Southern Hospital Conference, a conference for all of the hospitals in the south. While walking around with my hospital administrator and our architect, we ran into Linda's boss, Gary Strack, whom I knew as the administrator of Orange Memorial. As Linda happened to be with him, we were "reintroduced." Interestingly, no bells went off in my head when we met again; I only noticed how cute she was, and at that moment, I didn't remember having met her before. Later that afternoon, I headed to a function being held on top of Stone Mountain, hosted by one of the supply purveyors. To get there, we had to take a bus, and while walking down the aisle of the bus, I saw Linda sitting next to Gary. But this time, the bells went off, and I knew exactly who she was.

I said, "Didn't I meet you recently at Mac Davidson's house?"

She said, "Yeah, I think we did."

Walking back to my seat, I thought, "I must not have been very memorable that night." Since I was drinking that evening, I had an excuse for why I did not immediately remember her, but she wasn't drinking. What was her excuse? To this day, I don't know if she was just pretending not to know me, and even when I ask now, more than 45 years later, she still won't spill the beans.

It was chilly on top of the mountain, so I offered Linda my sports coat, which she accepted. When the evening was winding down and we started heading back to the bus, I didn't want the night to end. So I asked her, "Would you like to have a drink when we get back?"

She said, "No, thank you."

I countered, "Well, would you like to have a cup of coffee?"

She said, "No, thank you."

"Would you like anything?" I said as my last Hail Mary.

She said, "No, thank you."

I went on my merry way, but Linda had more than piqued my interest. She was attractive, smart, and hard to get. I was determined and loved a challenge, so when I returned to Orlando, I called her up to ask her to lunch, and she agreed!

On the day of our first date, I parked outside the hospital to pick her up. That was the first and last time I ever saw her in her "nurse whites." A couple of days after that lunch, we went to dinner. Then, we proceeded to go out eight days in a row. Then, Linda cut it off. She had a big job and wasn't looking for a distraction, and I was certainly a distraction. What she wanted was a career, not me—at this time anyway. This created a heightened challenge because, back then, there were no cell phones. If I called the hospital, there were maybe 12 people between her and the phone to keep her from taking my call, and as such, she ignored me for about a week. Ultimately, she gave in again, and I am so happy that I was persistent. I must have known that I was fighting for the life we have now.

By the end of 1977, our relationship became more serious. Later that winter, I took her to a Winter Park pizza joint called Sir Pizza. I didn't have a ring or anything, but I asked her to marry me. More or less, her response was, "Let me think about it." After hearing that, I wasn't sure what to do, for I had never asked anyone to marry me before. I didn't know what the protocol was when it came to a "waiting period." Did she have 10 hours to decide or two weeks? Thankfully, she gave me her answer one week later, and said yes!

On May 12, 1978, I married Linda Wilson. I had been in real estate for four years, but I didn't start Keewin until November of 1978. Essentially, I was a struggling guy in the real estate business trying to make it, and she was well-established in her career and job, making far more money than me at the hospital. I joke that I married her for her money. The joke became funnier when, six months after we were married, she quit her job. Needless to say, it worked out, and I went to work in earnest.

Linda had a small family: just one brother, like me. Also, both of our fathers worked in the grocery business in the meat department. With similar upbringings, it was always a given that we would have kids.

Our first daughter, Kinsley Sue, was born in 1981. Our second daughter, Kristen Enright, was born in 1986. Sue is Linda's middle name, and Enright is my middle name. So since

I couldn't have a Junior, we ended up with an Enright. Enright was also my grandmother's maiden name, and now our oldest grandchild is Annabelle Enright.

Kinsley was born with special needs, though we didn't know it for the first year of her life. We also didn't find out exactly what her condition was until she was 14. Kinsley couldn't walk, talk, or feed herself, and she had many seizures. But she was a very happy girl—very social, giggling and hugging everyone. We were extremely fortunate that Linda had an extensive medical background. Because of this, instead of not knowing what to do, Kinsley's level of care was significantly better than it would have been otherwise.

Linda went all over the country trying to figure out what caused Kinsley's condition: to the Children's Hospital in Boston, the National Cerebral Palsy Institute at the University of Iowa, the University of Virginia Medical Center, and Nemours Children's Hospital in Jacksonville. When Kinsley was 14, we finally met a doctor based in Melbourne who suspected what Kinsley had. He diagnosed her with a rare genetic disorder, Angelman syndrome (AS).

Angelman syndrome is named after Harry Angelman, a doctor in England who discovered the condition.[1] It is caused by a deficit of chromosome number 15 and "causes delayed development, problems with speech and balance, mental disability, and sometimes, seizures."[2] It turned out that Kinsley was previously tested for AS, but she was misdiagnosed. We also discovered that while we were scouring the country for an answer to her condition, there had been three national Angelman conferences here in Orlando. We had no idea.

Once we knew that Kinsley had AS, everything became clearer. We were able to give her the right medications for her seizures, some of which were the exact opposite of the meds she had been taking. It was an enormous relief to be able to give her appropriate care and, more than that, to learn that she had a full life expectancy. Although there is currently no cure for Angelman syndrome, scientists are very close to finding one because they have discovered the gene that causes AS.[3]

Our younger daughter, Kristen, was an active little girl who loved her sister very much. In fact, for her college essay, Kristen wrote about Kinsley. The essay acknowledged that she had a sister who was different. She talked about going to the mall or the movies and how, since Kinsley used a wheelchair, people would stare at her. Kristen ended the essay by conveying the fact that when she was younger, she thought that there was something wrong with her sister, but she later figured out that, really, there was something wrong with these other people who made her sister feel different. I read it and was filled with pride. I thought it was very poignant and right on.

Kristen was very smart and good in school. She was enrolled in IB courses at Winter Park High School as well as an active member of the marching band. Of course, I wanted her academic career to continue at Rollins. When she graduated high school in 2004, I was even willing to go so far as to bribe her to attend my alma mater. But she was stubborn, like her dad, and knew what she wanted. She attended American University in Washington, DC, and earned a dual degree in international relations and political science. She proceeded to do amazing things, later earning her master's degree in European economic policy from University College Dublin. About six years ago, she got married, and to my absolute delight, she and her husband, Dave, moved from Boston to Winter Park where they live with their two children, Annabelle and Anthony.

My grandchildren bring me more joy than anything. Annabelle is four and a half, and Anthony is two and a half. They are great kids and full of what I call "bug juice and vinegar." Anthony never learned to walk; he only learned to run. He comes into my office, looks at all of the senseless junk I have everywhere, and is totally content spending his time picking up everything and putting it down, one by one. Everything. Pick it up. Put it down. Pick it up. Put it down. And he is thoroughly entertained.

Annabelle is a little princess. When Dave's teaching Anthony to make muscles, Annabelle isn't interested at all and instead simply says, "I'm just beautiful." When anyone asks what she wants to be when she grows up, she responds, "Something pink and fabulous." We've got our hands full, but they are exceptional.

Kristen is president of my other business entity, Keewin LLC (my investment company, non-real estate), and vice president of Enright Real Property Company, her husband's company. She is also the co-trustee of our estate, and someday, when we have funded our family charitable foundation, she will be in charge of that. Her husband, Dave, was in the recruiting business in Boston, but when they decided to move here, he worked at Keewin for about two years. Then, because he needed a broader background and experience, he went to work for the nation's largest home builder, D.R. Horton. And less than a year ago, he went out on his own to establish Enright Real Property Company. Now, he's doing exactly what we do, creating residential communities throughout Central Florida and doing quite well.

With Kinsley and Kristen both living five minutes from our home, we see them often. Linda now serves as the "executive nanny" for Annabelle and Anthony, and we wouldn't want it any other way. When it comes to family, I can say with confidence, conviction, and pride that everyone is happy and doing well. And in the end, that is all you ever really need or could hope for. Family relationships are the most worth having and by far the best deal you could ever make.

AFTERWORD

Over the course of my career, a handful of people have told me that I should write a book. While I consider myself a good writer when drafting letters or legal documents, I never thought I would start, let alone finish, a book. Each time someone suggested this, I questioned the reasoning. If I wrote a book, what would it be about? If it detailed the events of my life or career, would it not be seen as egotistical? And would I have anything to share *worth reading*? Even after completing *Relationships and Reputation*, I still grapple with these questions.

Now, at the end of the process, I discovered that it takes more than ego to see a book through completion. It requires commitment, diligence, and above all else, a persistent reason to continue. From the beginning, my singular purpose has been to highlight the value of contributing to one's community and the value of relationships, not only in business but in life. My hope is that, amidst a rapidly changing social and political climate, young people may use these two universal principles—relationships and reputation—as the foundations for their futures, no matter how the world around them evolves.

Some say the days of company loyalty have ended and that the upcoming generation is not interested in dedicating 30 to 40 years of their lives to one employer. Many news outlets spread the narrative that young people are entitled: They wish to stay home and work, and they lack work ethic. This is a disjointed view with a great amount of nuance, and while I am no expert in the matter and cannot provide an in-depth analysis to the contrary, I do have faith in the young generation. In fact, I see a bit of myself in them.

When I founded The Keewin Real Property Company, I, like many young people today, did not want to work for anybody else. I guess I had some kind of burning internal entrepreneurial spirit—I liked the challenge. I liked making money. I liked being on my own, even though I have always had a partner in some way. More than anything, it's got to be fun. And with residential subdivision projects, which is the vast majority of our business, every deal is a little bit different.

I talk to many recent graduates as well as those just entering the real estate industry, and I most often say that I had a reason for the path I chose. There are a variety of product types one can pursue in real estate, and every one of them is different. For example, if you choose to go into real estate management, you would not be in investment sales. Similarly, if you go into development, you would not also be in management. This industry is unique in the way it is tailorable to one's specific interests, all while being a sustainable, lucrative career option. The best investment one can make is in land, and it is due to two reasons: scarcity and sustainability.

The real estate industry does have the inherent risk of market shifts. One of the most interesting parts of writing this book and reflecting on the past 50 years has been seeing the impact of economic upswings and downturns throughout my career from a 30,000-foot view. I often say that in real estate, there will always be times when you "can't sell an ice cube to an Inuit," meaning that no matter how smart you are or how great a piece of property is, you will sometimes not be able to make a deal work. The solution to this is being prepared with protections in place and refraining from overextending yourself. Many careers have been hindered by excessive optimism—that is, believing that a good cycle will never end and, therefore, not planning for this outcome.

As much as this risk requires careful decision-making, it is also what drew me to real estate in the first place. No one in my family had ever been to college, much less started a business. I like to say there was not an entrepreneurial bone in anyone's body. Meanwhile, I did everything entrepreneurial. Every dollar I have made has come from a deal, and because of this, I have not had a single W-2 paycheck since December 15, 1973. I am grateful to have been involved in approximately 20,000 residential lots across Central Florida as a developer or partner and to have driven community impact via my community board and political involvements.

One specific moment includes being the only Orlando-based entrepreneur to ever be featured in the most prominent section of the *Wall Street Journal*: on the front page, in the top right corner above the fold. The article was written by Tom Ricks, now a two-time winner of the Pulitzer Prize, and ran in both the national and international editions. In the article, I was described as a "small-time real estate developer" who "makes big-time money," the secret of which is the "network [I have] spent two decades building" and a "reputation for performance." Even in 1986, when the article was published, relationships and reputation clearly defined my success.

In addition to the *WSJ* article, several other highlights of my career and life are worth mentioning, such as helping raise $500,000 to rescue the still-flourishing *Winter Park Magazine* and contributing to the establishment of Rollins College's first Colloquy in 2007, an event that brought in world-famous speakers like Maya Angelou, George Takei, Jane Goodall, and Sally Ride, among others. Keewin's office is full of mementos from these exploits, as well as others mentioned in this book such as having the original printing plates used for the *WSJ* article, the paper that I used to write down Nelson Schwab's contact information for Universal Studios, and my first office "desk." Perhaps my most proud momento, though, is a framed document and medal in my office that reads in large, red letters, "FRANCISCVS PONT. MAX." This document tends to raise eyebrows and draw questions, to which I explain that it represents one of my most prized accomplishments and honors received.

In 2008, I became very involved in my local Catholic church and diocese. I have been a practicing Catholic my entire life, but at that time, I became a more active parishioner at St. Margaret Mary Catholic Church in Winter Park. The prior year, the diocese had formed a "synod," a planning process that establishes approximately 30 groups to improve different programs of the church. These groups researched topics such as attendance, outreach programs, governance, and others. The synod also chose to recommend the establishment of a charitable foundation as part of the diocese called the Catholic Foundation of Central Florida, with the intention of initially raising $150 million in a diocese-wide capital campaign. Linda and I made a contribution soon after its establishment, and I was asked at the same time to serve as a member of the foundation board and serve as the second chairman of the board of directors from 2010 to 2013.

I became more involved in the diocese, and subsequently, I was appointed to the debt reduction committee. I also chaired the real estate committee, among other activities. In one important transaction, the church encountered a significant issue when attempting to sell a major piece of property. The two people managing this sale were a CPA and a lawyer, and as it turned out, they did not have the experience in real estate and related politics to execute the deal and allow the diocese to receive the full value of the property, which was well into the millions. The bishop of Orlando recognized the severity of the situation and, knowing that I had been active in the real estate business for years, approached me for assistance. At the beginning of the prior process, the diocese was told to expect $16 million for the property, but only if all the risks involved did not lower that profit. In addition, the diocese would have to wait a number of years to receive any payment.

Using some of my real estate contacts, after the original process was terminated by the bishop, we secured a new real estate contract for the property that closed for $26 million, all cash, less than half a year later—a significant turn of events. Normally, the decision to proceed with a transaction of this size had to be approved by several different internal committees and church leaders before going all the way to Rome for final approval. This was because, for any Catholic Church property worth more than a million dollars, no matter where in the world, the church in Rome had to approve a sale.

Fortunately, the bishop, whom I am still close to, was astute enough to abandon this "normal" process. Instead, the bishop requested that I go directly to the board of electors, effectively bypassing every other part of the process that would typically be needed. I was asked to go directly to the top, where the decision was made to proceed with the sale. Afterward, the bishop went back to the other parties for their consent, though the decision had already been made. This reflects the importance of this property sale and the significant impact it would have on the diocese's financial condition.

The Papal Order of St. Gregory the Great Certificate and Medal

I suppose it is for reasons like this that, unbeknownst to me, the diocese nominated me to be knighted to the Pontifical Equestrian Order of St. Gregory the Great. And, to my surprise, I received this award—a high honor that has only been bestowed upon a few hundred people since its creation in 1831.[1] Past recipients include Bob Hope, Roy Disney, and Walter Annenberg. The award ceremony was held at the Basilica of the National Shrine of Mary, Queen of the Universe, a beautiful shrine and church south of Orlando, and the bishop of Orlando, John Noonan, bestowed the honor to me on behalf of Pope Francis. In addition to the aforementioned certificate, I received a medal and a sword related to this honor.

It is interesting how fate works, how forks in the road take you to different places. Life comes with surprises, ups and downs, and factors outside of your control. When one encounters a setback, sometimes all you can do is take time to reflect and contemplate the missed opportunity and then find the motivation inside of yourself to identify a new solution. I have found that this approach is only possible through forming strong relationships with others and creating a reputation of community service and giving back. If you are someone just entering a career in real estate, or even someone who simply has an interest in doing so, I hope that after reading my story, you believe that following a similar fork in the road is possible for you as well.

I do not have any plans for retirement—one, because Linda does not really want me home all the time, and two, because I believe in the adage of "make hay while the sun shines" when it comes to the real estate industry. Instead of retiring, I look forward to continuing my work while doing more of what I love, including traveling, spending time with my family, and gathering friends at SweetPea, my unique cracker-style houseboat at the Sanford Marina. As for my many board and community involvements, I intend to continue helping where I can, but I also believe in getting out of the way so that other people can execute their visions and seize their own opportunities. I am happy to provide advice when needed, but I no longer feel the need to be at the front of the line.

In regards to "retirement," when that time comes, if I do nothing but come down to the office, sit on Keewin's front porch that overlooks Winter Park's Central Park, work a little, visit with friends, and watch the trains go by ... well, there is nothing wrong with that.

SweetPea, the Cracker-Style Houseboat

ACKNOWLEDGMENTS

Thanks to those of you who have been part of this journey:

Rollins College, for providing my "start."

Charlie Rice, for supporting and encouraging me early on.

Bill Bieberbach, for making that most special introduction to Universal Studios.

My brother Tim, along with your great partner and wife, **Marian**, who became my close friend when we moved to Puerto Rico and remained as such for the rest of your life.

Larry Godwin, for being my first loyal and solid partner and friend for so many years—the other half of the Keewin name.

Ed Leerdam, my Dutch partner for 12 years as EuroCapital Partners, with offices in Winter Park and The Hague, Netherlands. Together, we brought capital from Holland to our real estate deals and enjoyed, while it lasted, a great business and personal relationship . . . important to the foundation of my success.

Jay Folk, my second Keewin partner, who also became a very close personal friend. A great spirited and happy man, we did a lot of fun things together.

Rita Bornstein, for believing in me and standing behind me.

Steve Rosser and McKinzie Terrill, for being such important and supportive partners and my Keewin partners today. Truly a case of 1 + 1 + 1 = 10!

Sarah Sprinkel, for being a wonderful friend and neighbor with **George** at your side all those years. George is no longer with us, but his spirit remains. And, of course, for being Kinsley's godmother.

Warren and Marilyn Williams, for being such special friends, dinner-mates, and traveling buddies. Always there for us and always smiling.

Mason Blake, for being my Jaycee buddy and then becoming my close friend and attorney for many many years, including being the trustee of our estate planning entities with **Amy** at your side, the perfect Southern lady.

Jeffrey and Caroline Blydenburgh, the lucky folks who purchased the first lot and home in Windsong. From there, Jeffrey served as a valuable ally on the Homeowner's Association board, and over time, you have both been close friends and world-traveling companions of ours.

Orlando Evora, for being a most loyal and steadfast friend, a fellow board member of three major community organizations, and now, the co-trustee of our estate matters. Truly an exceptional personal friend.

Terry Hadley, the "world famous, gray-haired country lawyer" and my personal lawyer for over 30 years, for providing wise counsel through the good times and bad and being a dear friend.

Joe Swedish, for being my traveling partner and my most loyal investor, someone who took a job at our local hospital, Winter Park Memorial, and catapulted your career to become one of the top healthcare executives in the country.

Eric and Emma Mason, for starting as Kinsley's physical therapist. Eric, you soon became someone Kinsley loved dearly as you helped her to do amazing things. What's more, you and Emma allowed us to become part of your family, who live in the magical, tiny village of Tockholes in Lancashire, England. Friends forever.

Ken Meister, for being a great investment banker, private equity guy, and my close friend who enjoys exotic travel, cigars, and whiskey with me.

Jack Myers, a special fellow Crummer graduate. Great thanks for allowing me to join your family company's board of directors for over 20 years.

Rob and Carol Hille, for initially being fellow "band parents" with Linda and me, and then, Carol, for becoming Linda's very best personal friend. You are great folks and such good friends.

Cynthia and Phil Wood, whom I have known for more than 46 years—longer than I have been with Linda—for being close and special friends, and Cynthia, for being a special godmother to Kristen.

Brock Magruder, John Jennings, and Greg Hart, who shared the life-changing Cursillo spiritual experience together, reinforced by our weekly meetings since 2001—over 23 years.

Jim Barnes, for bringing me into the BankFIRST investment opportunity, allowing me to become a principal investor, and when there were tough times, standing by me and backing me all the way—a closer friend you could not have.

Jim Hansberger, another traveling friend and my financial advisor for over 30 years, who is smart, talented, and one more person who stuck with me. Even when I was not a financial contributor to your business, you were there to see me recover and benefit from your financial acumen for many, many years.

Grant Cornwell, with your partner and wife **Peg**, by far one of Rollins College's greatest presidents who I had the honor and pleasure to select for the job. You and Peg are leaving an incredible mark on the future of the college.

Toni Jennings, a most bright and exceptional leader, former two-term Florida Senate president, and Lt. Governor under Jeb Bush, for being a friend beyond belief, and most importantly, the person who single-handedly secured a place for Kinsley, our special needs daughter, at Howell Branch Court, her current home, for which we are eternally grateful.

Evan Dobelle, with one of his claims to fame being the chief of protocol with the Carter administration. Thank you for being my friend and allowing me to attend the famous Bohemian Grove in California, which I have been so very lucky to participate in for the last 20-plus years.

James and Sherry Cooper, for being trusted friends. As my special assistant for 24 years, Sherry, you took care of me and allowed me to do most of what I have accomplished. And James, thank you for serving as the manager of our residence building for many years. You are an excellent manager and a great person and friend protecting our interests.

Larry Martindale, the Waffle House man, and **Susan**, for always being there for support and friendship.

Ken Wright, my oldest friend going back to high school, for being loyal and fun to be with, and for introducing me to Sweet Pea, our unique cracker-style houseboat at the Sanford Marina.

Fr. Richard Walsh, my spiritual advisor, who has always been a guiding light and supporter. A special man . . .

My many fellow Rollins Trustees, for 36 years of doing good for the college—folks like **Ted and Barbara Alfond,** uber-philanthropic individuals and world-class art experts; **Harold Ward,** the wisest of them all, who trusted me with the precious asset that became Windsong; **Philip Tiedtke,** an exceptionally smart businessman; and bright and beautiful **Sig,** his wife, and with the family, the creator and sponsor of Enzian Theater, a treasure for Central Florida.

Richard Swann and his family, including Dorothy and Christian. It was Richard who involved me in the world of high-level politics and became my good friend, as well as the primary reason I succeeded early in the residential real-estate business by providing my first two development opportunities.

Heartfelt thanks to you all!

NOTES

Chapter Seven

1. "The History of Apopka," The Apopka Museum, accessed November 11, 2024, https://theapopkamuseum.com/history-of-apopka/.

Chapter Eight

1. Jonathan Kandell, "Lew Wasserman, 89, Is Dead; Last of Hollywood's Moguls," *The New York Times*, June 4, 2002, https://www.nytimes.com/2002/06/04/business/lew-wasserman-89-is-dead-last-of-hollywood-s-moguls.html.

Chapter Eleven

1. "Charles Hosmer Morse," The Charles Hosmer Morse Museum of American Art, accessed November 11, 2024, https://morsemuseum.org/morse-history/charles-hosmer-morse/.
2. "Trust History," Elizabeth Morse Genius Charitable Trust, accessed November 11, 2024, https://emgeniustrust.org/About-the-Trust/Trust-History.aspx.
3. Leslie Kemp Poole, "Winter Park's Genius Preserve," *From the Rollins Archives* (blog), April 21, 2023, https://blogs.rollins.edu/libraryarchives/2023/04/21/winter-parks-genius-preserve-a-short-history/.

Chapter Thirteen

1. Tom Huddleston Jr., "How Many Recessions You've Actually Lived Through and What Happened in Every One," CNBC, April 9, 2020, https://www.cnbc.com/2020/04/09/what-happened-in-every-us-recession-since-the-great-depression.html.
2. "Savings and Loan Crisis," Federal Reserve History, November 22, 2013, https://www.federalreservehistory.org/essays/savings-and-loan-crisis.
3. Sangkyun Park, "Why Did Thrift Goodwill Matter in 1989?" *Federal Reserve Bank of New York Paper Series*, no. 51 (November 1998): https://dx.doi.org/10.2139/ssrn.151308.
4. "Savings and Loan Crisis," Federal Reserve History, November 22, 2013, https://www.federalreservehistory.org/essays/savings-and-loan-crisis.
5. "American Pioneer Savings Bank," US Bank Locations, accessed November 11, 2024, https://www.usbanklocations.com/american-pioneer-savings-bank-32056.shtml.

Chapter Fourteen

1. "Wekiva River Aquatic Preserve," Florida Department of Environmental Protection, updated October 3, 2024, https://floridadep.gov/rcp/aquatic-preserve/locations/wekiva-river-aquatic-preserve.
2. "Wekiva River," National Wild and Scenic Rivers System, October 13, 2000, https://www.rivers.gov/river/wekiva.

Chapter Fifteen

1. Annie Martin, "Rita Bornstein, Former Rollins President Known for Fundraising Chops, Dies at 88," *Orlando Sentinel*, updated January 10, 2024, https://www.orlandosentinel.com/2024/01/10/rita-bornstein-former-rollins-president-known-for-fundraising-chops-dies-at-88/.
2. "About Harold Alfond," Harold Alfond Foundation, accessed November 11, 2024, https://www.haroldalfondfoundation.org/about-the-foundation/harold-alfond/.
3. Liam Taylor King, "A College Hotel? From the Langford to the Alfond (1956–2023)," *From the Rollins Archives* (blog), accessed November 11, 2024, https://blogs.rollins.edu/libraryarchives/2023/12/18/a-college-hotel-from-the-langford-to-the-alfond-1956-2023/.
4. "A Work of Heart," The Alfond Inn, accessed November 11, 2024, https://thealfondinn.com/winter-park/history.
5. "Alfond Scholars Program," Rollins, accessed November 11, 2024, https://www.rollins.edu/scholarships-aid/scholarships/alfond-scholars-program/.
6. Stephanie Rizzo, "The Alfond Inn Named No. 2 Hotel in Florida," Rollins, October 20, 2022, https://www.rollins.edu/news/the-alfond-inn-named-no-2-hotel-in-florida/.

Chapter Eighteen

1. "What Is Angelman Syndrome," Angelman Syndrome Foundation, accessed November 11, 2024, https://www.angelman.org/what-is-as/.

2. "Angelman Syndrome," Mayo Clinic, March 8, 2024, https://www.mayoclinic.org/diseases-conditions/angelman-syndrome/symptoms-causes/syc-20355621.

3. "What Is Angelman Syndrome," Angelman Syndrome Foundation, accessed November 11, 2024, https://www.angelman.org/what-is-as/.

Afterword

1. "The Papal Order of Saint Gregory the Great," The Christian Knighthood Information Center, accessed November 11, 2024, https://www.papalknights.org/greg.html.

ABOUT THE AUTHOR

Allan E. Keen is the chairman, founder, and CEO of The Keewin Real Property Company, a real estate development, investment, brokerage, and consulting company located in Winter Park, Florida.

Founded in 1978, Keewin has entitled, developed, and/or marketed over 20,000 single-family and townhome residential lots, making the company one of the largest residential lot developers in Central Florida. Notable deals include acting as the exclusive real estate broker for Universal Studios Florida for 20 years and developing the Windsong residential community in Winter Park. Keen and Keewin have been involved in over $900 million worth of real estate transactions since the company's formation.

Elected to the Rollins College Board of Trustees in 1988, Keen served as chairman of the board from 2006 to 2008 and from 2015 to 2019 and is currently the longest-serving Board of Trustees member. From 2014 to 2015, Keen was chairman of the search committee for the 15th president of Rollins College, Grant Cornwell, and previously chaired the search committee that brought Rita Bornstein to Rollins as its 13th president.

Keen is a current or former board member for a number of organizations in a wide range of industries, including Winter Park Publishing Company, the Catholic Foundation of Central Florida, Inc., BankFIRST, and No Labels, among others. He has been appointed to public board positions by two notable political figures: once in 2001 by Governor Jeb Bush to the Orlando-Orange County Expressway Authority Board of Directors, and again in 2019 by Orange County Mayor Jerry Demings as co-chair of his Housing For All task force.

Keen received his bachelor of arts degree in economics from Rollins College and an MBA from the Roy E. Crummer Graduate School of Business at Rollins. In 2010, an Honorary Doctor of Humane Letters (DHL) degree was awarded to Keen at the college's annual commencement. In 2018, Keen also received the Knight of the Pontifical Equestrian Order of St. Gregory the Great award, conferred by Pope Francis and presented by Bishop John Noonan of Orlando.

Keen resides in Winter Park with his wife, two daughters, and two grandchildren and is a member of St. Margaret Mary Catholic Church.

www.ingramcontent.com/pod-product-compliance
Lightning Source LLC
Chambersburg PA
CBHW050733010526
44107CB00010B/832